THE RADICALS' CITY:
URBAN ENVIRONMENT, POLARISATION, COHESION

To all who realise that matter matters,
including Julia, Matilda and Adam.

The Radicals' City:
Urban Environment, Polarisation, Cohesion

Ralf Brand
University of Manchester, UK

Sara Fregonese
University of Birmingham, UK

ASHGATE

Published by
Ashgate Publishing Limited
Wey Court East
Union Road
Farnham
Surrey, GU9 7PT
England

Ashgate Publishing Company
110 Cherry Street
Suite 3-1
Burlington, VT 05401-3818
USA

www.ashgate.com

British Library Cataloguing in Publication Data
A catalogue record for this book is available from the British Library.

The Library of Congress has cataloged the printed edition as follows:
Brand, Ralf.
 The radicals' city : urban environment, polarisation, cohesion / by Ralf Brand and Sara Fregonese.
     pages cm. -- (Design and the built environment)
 Includes bibliographical references and index.
 ISBN 978-1-4094-5160-0 (hardback) -- ISBN 978-1-4094-5161-7 (ebook) -- ISBN 978-1-4094-7275-9 (epub) 1. Urbanization--Social aspects.
2. Polarization (Social sciences) 3. Intergroup relations. 4. Urban policy. 5. Sociology, Urban. I. Fregonese, Sara. II. Title.
 HT151.B643 2013
 307.76--dc23
                                                                            2012045466
ISBN 9781409451600 (hbk)
ISBN 9781409451617 (ebk – PDF)
ISBN 9781409472759 (ebk – ePUB)

Printed in the United Kingdom by Henry Ling Limited, at the Dorset Press, Dorchester, DT1 1HD

Contents

List of Figures

List of Maps

Notes on Contributors

At the time of writing and during the research project upon which this book is based **Ralf Brand** was Senior Lecturer in Architectural Studies at the Manchester Architecture Research Centre, University of Manchester, UK. In his PhD in Community and Regional Planning (2003) he developed the notion of a 'synchronisation' of social and technical (or material) change. Since then, he applied this conceptual angle for a variety of substantive issues like contested cities, multi-faith spaces, green architecture or sustainable mobility. The latter is his current main area of work after his move to Rupprecht Consult in Cologne, Germany.

Sara Fregonese is Birmingham Fellow in the School of Geography, Earth, and Environmental Sciences and a member of the Institute for Conflict, Cooperation and Security at the University of Birmingham. At the time of writing, she was British Academy Post-Doctoral Fellow at Royal Holloway University of London. In her doctoral and post-doctoral research on urban space and political violence in Lebanon, she developed the concept of 'hybrid sovereignty' to consider the interactions between classical state actors and non-state groups in the control of political violence, territory and infrastructure. She applies hybrid sovereignty to international politics as an alternative approach to so-called 'fragile' and 'weak' states; to urban community relations, radicalisation and conflict, and to post-uprising transition.

Acknowledgements

As with most books, this one would not have been possible with the crucial, generous and friendly support by many people, whose name does not appear on the cover. In our case, we happily admit that even the underlying research project would not have been possible without many other collaborators. In fact, the bid would not even have been written without the encouragement and help of others. We would therefore like to express our sincere gratitude to the following persons:

Co-Investigator, Prof. Jon Coaffee; also author of our epilogue.
Director of the *New Security Challenges Programme*, Prof. Stuart Croft.

Advisory Council Members

Dr Thomas Bürk (Ethnology, back then at the Institute for Regional Development and Structural Planning, Erkner near Berlin), expert on right-wing extremism in large residential blocks.
Prof. Rachid Chamoun (Urban Design, Lebanese American University), Director of the Lebanese Urban Planning Institute.
Prof. Frank Gaffikin (Spatial Planning, Queen's University Belfast), expertise in spatio-political implications of contestation.
Prof. Simon Guy (Sociologist, University of Manchester), Director of the Manchester Architecture Research Centre.
Prof. Maarten Hajer (Public Policy, University of Amsterdam), Co-Initiator of the Amsterdam Centrum for Conflict Studies.
Dr Maarten Poorter (Political Science, University of Amsterdam), expert in Conflict Studies and Public Participation.
Dr Wendy Pullan (Architecture, University of Cambridge), Principal Investigator of *Conflict in Cities and the Contested State*.

Exhibition Designers

Wolfgang Obermair. Artist and curator. Assistant Professor at the University of
    Applied Arts Vienna in the Department for Transmedial Art.
Andrea Börner, Lecturer at the University of Applied Arts Vienna in the Institute for
    Architecture.

Interviewees for Chapter 9

Prof. Frank Gaffikin (see above).
Prof. Wendy Pullan (see above).
Jon Calame (Minerva Partners), co-author of *Divided Cities: Beirut, Belfast, Jerusalem,
    Mostar and Nicosia.*
Prof. Scott Bollens (Urban Planning, University of California, Irvine), Professor of
    Peace and International Cooperation.

*Leaders of the participatory data gathering projects and their anonymous volunteers,
who documented their everyday urban environment for us with disposable cameras
and mental maps:*

Dr Christine Lasch and her students in the advanced course *Politische Weltkunde*
    (Understanding the Political World), Manfred von Ardenne Gymnasium, Berlin.
Caroline Murphy and her collaborators and participants in the project 'Picture This'
    from the Suffolk and Lenadoon Interface Group, Belfast.
Frouke Russchen and the participants in her youth group in Slootervaart,
    Amsterdam.
Prof. Leon Telvizian and his students in Urban Planning at the Université Libanaise
    de Beyrouth, Département d'Urbanisme, Beirut.

The cover image was designed by Victor Chapartegui from graffiti4hire®, who
kindly agreed to help us with this academic book project for a really fair price.
Highly recommended!
    And many thanks to the following colleagues, friends, interviewees,[1] participants,
admin support staff, staff at Ashgate and others who share a common point with
this interdisciplinary book by not falling into neat pre-established categories. In
alphabetical order and without their academic titles:

Bachir Abou Mounsef; James Anderson; Anonymous Police Officer from the Police
Station at Allebeplein, Slotervaart; Anonymous users of the 'Liebenwalder Garten'
(Berlin); Anonymous users of the synagogue on Fasanenstrasse (Berlin); Apabiz;
Moustapha Baba; Nadine Badr; Edwin Bakker; Gail Barbour; Ediens Bartels; Carolin
Behrens; Carsten Betzner; Bradley Biggerstaff; Wiebe Bijker; Klaas Bindert de Haan;

---

1   Please note that we provide only the names of those interviewees who have explicitly
agreed to the disclosure of their real names. All others are referred to by pseudonyms in the
book but not mentioned here.

Dierk Borstel; Tamara Boyle; Colm Bradley; Rachel Briggs; Jean Brown; Nicole Campbell; Jack Cassidy; Wissam Chaaya; Youssef Chaitani; Esther Charlesworth; Zaher Chatila; Florencio Chicote; Jude Chillman; Carl Chung; Alex Clarke; Gemma Clarke; Pollyanna Clayton Stamm; Simon Colwill; Sarah Connolly; Mel Corry; Carolyn Court; Renee Crawford; Malisah Crothers; Azucena Cruz; Maaike Dautzenberg; Pi De Bruijn; Edith De Graaf; Orlaigh Deacon; Gerard Deery; Froukje Demant; Shannon Donnan; Sher Doruff; Isabelle Doucet; Sammy Douglas; Matthias Dunken; Julia Eischer; Volker Eick; Hussein El Husseini; Hisham Elkadi; Conor Ellis; Martin Ellis; ESRC; Lucas Evers; Macy Ewart; Mona Fawaz; Jan Fischer; Vanessa Fischer; Katharina Fleischmann; Debbie Flynn; Hermann Gabler; Emma Gallon; Norbert Gebauer; Dirk Gebhardt; Caroline Gibson; Jonathan Githens-Mazer; Dick Glastra Van Loon; Sylvia Gordon; Rupert Griffiths; Michael Hall; Atef Hamdy; Mona Harb; Marie-Therese Harrand; Damien Harte; Robyn Hartley; Marian Hawkesworth; Jennifer Hawthorne; Michael Hebbert; Zef Hemel; Chris Hewson; Michael Hodge; John Hoey; Andrej Holm; Hoteliers in Belfast, Berlin and Amsterdam; Will Hurst; Rachid Jalkh; Sany Jamal; Joost Janmaat; Neil Jarman; Maria Kaika; Andrew Karvonen; Andy Kennedy; Karsten Ketzner; Al-Hajj Said Khansa; Ralf Knoche; Marie Louise Knox; Frank Kresin; Sabine Kritter; Miodrag Kuc; Christine Lasch; Claire Launchbury; Maaike Lauwaert; Kyle Laverty; Kirstie Lavery; Lynette Lee; Jill Lee-Borrett; Guenther Lewanzik; Alan Lewis; Simona Loi; Cordula Looid-Reisch; Claudia Luzar; Ciaran Mackel; Michael Mallé; Melissa Mallon; Virginie Mamadouh; Antoine Mansour; Robert Mason; Heike Marqardt; Caoimhe McAuley; Aine McCabe; Conor McCafferty; Breigeann McCann; Hugh McCloskey; Declan McCreesh; Stephen McCusker; Sarah Maria McDonald; Roisin McFarlane; Cortney McKeown; Keileigh McKeown; Mary McKeown; Darren McKinley; Louise McNeill; Guus Meijer; Collin Mellis; Jürgen Metzech; Leandro Minuchin; Suzanne Mol; Bill Morrison; Ruth Morrow; Timothy Moss; Bachir Moujaes; Mounira al Solh; Ziad Moutran; Caroline Murphy; Danielle Murray; Seaneen Murray; Brendan Murtagh; Caroline Nevedjan; Elma Newberry; Stephen Nolan; Liam O'Dowd; Chris O'Halloran; Paul O'Hare; Clodagh O'Rourke; Etain O'Rourke; Orient Institut Beirut; Chris Paris; Britney Patrick; Iris Plate; Lizette Ploeg; Eva Prausner; Mark Rainey; Adam Ramadan; Valerie Rose; Frouke Russchen; Robert Saliba; Stephen Salley; Martin Schäfer; Claudia Schmid; David Shervington; Ian Shuttleworth; Magda Sibley; Cora-Yfke Sikkema; Jan Simons; Marieke Slootman; Nadine Smyth; Amira Solh; Jack Spence; Sam Stanex; Ken Sterret; Rüdiger Suppin; William Stewart; Tjil Sunier; Ewan Suttie; Bjoern Swijekowsky; Aouatif Tawfik; Francis Teeney; Leon Telvizian; Saskia Tempelman; Jean Tillie; Paula Tolan; Amberlea Trainor; Fadi Tufayli; Justus Uitermark; Charles van den Heuvel; Eric van der Kooij; Bas van Heur; Rob van Kranenburg; Tijs van Maasakkers; Paul van Soomeren; Sacha van Tongeren; Nanke Verloo; Flores Vermeulen; Andreas Wächter; Jürgen Weidinger; Debra Whitehead; Caroline Wilson; Heiko Wimmen; Tobias Woldendorp; Chris Wyatt; Rachel Wyatt; Sally Wyatt; Albena Yaneva; Sayyed Yasser El Mousawi; Nico Zimmermann.

In addition we would like to thank the many individuals who agreed to be interviewed by us but chose not to have their real names disclosed. As expressed in our Informed Consent Agreement with them we fully understand and respect their decision but would nevertheless express our gratitude in this way.

We also would like to thank those whose name we could not or forgot to record.

Given the sensitive nature of the issues addressed in this book we also would like to apologise in advance to anyone who might feel misrepresented in our account, whose property might be visible in certain photographs and therefore appear in a negative light or who feel treated unfairly in any other way. Please rest assured that we followed the principle of due diligence to check the factual accuracy of our statements. We may have, however, been misinformed ourselves or – despite all our best efforts – simply be wrong. For these cases we would like to apologise in advance and ask you to contact us so that we can publish any corrigenda on the project website www.urbanpolarisation.org.

Unless mentioned otherwise the copyright for all images is held by Ralf Brand and Sara Fregonese. We would like to manage expectations about the technical quality of some photographs in this book. Due to the nature of its topic we simply could not take photographs as carefully as we would have liked in many places.

In fact, on some occasions it would have been insensitive or outright dangerous to take pictures in a relaxed tourist mode. In some cases we had to, literally, shoot from the hip. And where images were taken by our volunteers in one of our four 'participatory photo documentation projects' we obviously could not control the image quality. As we will explain later, some of these images were taken with disposable cameras, which we provided as part of our participatory data-gathering methodology. What counts is the content of the pictures.

List of Abbreviations and Acronyms

ANT	Actor-Network Theory
AHRC	Arts and Humanities Research Council
BCD	Beirut Central District
CCTV	Closed Circuit Television
CPTED	Crime Prevention Through Environmental Design
DFPNI	Department of Finance and Personnel, Northern Ireland
EASST	European Association for the Study of Science and Technology
ESCWA	Economic and Social Commission for Western Asia
ESRC	Economic and Social Research Council
FCO	Foreign and Commonwealth Office
GAA	Gaelic Athletic Association
IRA	Irish Republican Army
MARC	Manchester Architecture Research Centre
NISRA	Northern Ireland Statistics and Research Agency
NIO	Northern Ireland Office
NPD	Nationaldemokratische Partei Deutschlands
OED	*Oxford English Dictionary*
RQ	Research Question
RUSI	Royal United Services Institute
SCOT	Social Construction of Technology
SRRP	Stewartstown Road Regeneration Project
STS	Science and Technology Studies

1

Introduction

The city is neither a background to these struggles *against which* groups wager, nor is it a foreground *for which* groups struggle for domination. The city is the battleground *through which* groups define their identities, stake their claims, wage their battles, and articulate citizenship rights and obligations (Isin 2002: 50).

BACKGROUND

The argument in this book is that polarisation (or even radicalisation) and cohesion are not only mental phenomena inside people's heads. They also 'take place', literally. They happen *somewhere*, mostly in a particular urban environment. You could even point out polarisation-related places on a map.

We argue that polarised (or divided[1]) cities like Belfast, Beirut, Mostar, Jerusalem, Nicosia – but also cities widely recognised as 'peaceful' like Paris, Chicago and London – feature spatial, architectural and infrastructural implications and expressions of polarising or radicalising socio-political conditions – what we call 'mirrors' of polarisation. These range from clear-cut segregation through walls, fences and the duplication of services and infrastructures, to subtler or codified territorial markers like painted kerb stones and graffiti, to dramatic and ephemeral phenomena like public protests, encampments and violent riots.

Conversely, the material make-up of cities can also exert an intended or unintended agency, like a gravitational pull upon social practices. For example, perceptions of urban safety, daily rituals like choosing shopping locations or commuting routes, preferences for a particular playground, the generation or

---

1   While there is increasing literature on divided cities, there is also a lack of consistency in the definition and use of this concept. Gaffikin and Morrisey (2011: 55) thus argue that the slogan of the divided city is 'as ambiguous, as it is ubiquitous'. Their attempt to remedy this situation is a suggested categorisation of eight types of urban division (Chapter 2 and Chapter 4).

perpetuation of suspicion and prejudices but also the likelihood of meeting others, the conviviality of spaces and their suitability for sharing can be conditioned and solidified by all kinds of urban artefacts. For example, after consultations with local planning institutions and the police, recently the UK government abandoned plans to ease planning restrictions for those shopkeepers who wish to install security shutters in their shops in certain areas of London affected by the 2011 riots. The reason for the change of plans is the fear of a counter-productive overreaction: 'Police and councils advised that relaxing these [planning] rules could have the opposite effect and increase crime and anti-social behaviour by giving High Streets [sic] the appearance of being under siege' (BBC News 2012). Even more recently, a row of shops in riot-hit South-East London had their shutters painted with faces of local babies by a collective of graffiti artists. The intention is – in the correspondent's words – 'to try and use the environment to moderate behaviour', deterring vandalism and promoting feelings of care and belonging in local passersby (Gordon 2012). We understand these and similar processes as the 'mediating' effect of the urban environment. If it is true that tangible elements of a city can have an influence not only on mundane aspects of people's life, but even on the process of polarisation itself, then a better understanding of this process could potentially help prevent deterioration or contribute to an improvement of the situation. In a nutshell, social conditions and urban environments shape each other, and we compared this dynamic between the social and the material in four different cities with substantially different types of polarisation – and in some cases even radicalisation – and with a number of attempts to achieve a more cohesive urban society (see Chapter 2 for a more detailed description of the underlying research project).

There is growing appreciation and an increasing body of literature studying the material aspects of open and/or declared conflict in urban contexts: An emblematic case is Israel/Palestine, and other extreme ones are Belfast or Nicosia during the heydays of division. What differentiates the research underlying this book (see Chapter 2), instead, is a focus on the early stages, the less dramatic but crucial spatial contexts of growing, developing polar*isation* (and equally attempts of de-polar*isation*) rather than polar*ised* situations.[2] This accent on the *process* of polarisation rather than on the *state* of polarisation as a given, 'black-boxed' condition of a city, allowed us to highlight the everyday dynamics by which people grow apart or come together in cities. By opening this black box, we found busy engine rooms of socio-material urban processes of division and attempts at cohesion.

The approach in this book also tackles what we call a socio-material blind spot in studies on radicalisation and polarisation. While the literature on social cohesion,

---

2   Noteworthy in this respect is the project 'Understanding the urban tipping point', also conducted at the University of Manchester. This study asks 'how, why, and under what circumstances the conflict inherent to city living can tip over into generalised violence' (www.urbantippingpoint.org).

polarisation and even radicalisation is vast and interdisciplinary (see Chapter 3), the academic and practical engagement with such themes has been so far mostly the traditional remit of sociologists, historians, psychologists, political scientists and conflict resolution specialists. In other terms, the study of radicalisation is predominantly populated by scholars and professionals addressing the political, social and behavioural aspects of the issue. Despite this predominance, an increasing number of scholars from disciplines such as architecture, urban studies and planning have begun to focus on the spatial and material angles of these phenomena, mostly on the ways in which conflict materialises in all kinds of urban technologies of partition. Both social and material aspects are crucial for the everyday reality of polarised societies, but it takes more than the presence of two topically similar but theoretically and methodologically disconnected perspectives to understand polarising cities. The intimate links between social and material sides of polarisation deserve a more symbiotic consideration than is conventionally acknowledged: An integrated approach within the same research process (Bijker 1992) that brings together in the same study what has so far been done separately by studies specialising in *either* the social *or* in the material aspects of contestation. This book adopts precisely this much needed stereoscopic approach: It tunes into *both* the social *and* the material, highlighting the 'socio-materiality' of polarisation (and in the same way, de-polarisation and cohesion).

TERMINOLOGY

Social polarisation and cohesion are extremely complex and inherently sensitive processes that involve the everyday life of potentially many thousands people in their urban surroundings. It is crucial therefore to define or at least discuss critically the terms and concepts that the title of this project engages with.

Urban Environment

Everything material and/or built that constitutes our cities, from large infrastructures (street layouts, transport infrastructure, parks, buildings, playgrounds …) to individual artefacts (walls and fences, benches, bollards, flags, plants, windows …), interacts with human activity.

Mirror

This project is based on the assumption that the urban environment mirrors certain social, political and/or economic conditions like tension, polarisation and even radicalisation. A critical look at the materiality of a city can tell us a lot about the processes happening within it. Our research aimed to better understand how social and political conditions get manifested by or translated into the urban environment.

Mediator

Among the various definitions of the verb 'to mediate', the most relevant one here is 'to intercede or intervene' (OED Online 2012a). The urban environment not only mirrors but can also mediate social conditions. It constantly influences the ways in which daily lives are acted out: A closed park can change the destination of our Sunday walk, traffic diversions change our commuting routes, a dark street changes walking routes at night or even the possibility to walk alone. However, the built environment does not only change our corporeal behaviour and mobility. We investigated the possibility that the built environment also intervenes to change perceptions, shaping and possibly even perpetuating stereotypes about other social, ethnic, religious, political groups and the (un-)likeliness of friendly encounters with them.

This position is not a crude form of material determinism or an endorsement of blunt social engineering. Of course we realise that knocking down a fence will not automatically make people like each other. But likewise, we cannot simply preach neighbourliness between warring social groups when a wall literally prevents visual and acoustic encounters. What we want to communicate with the notion of the urban environment as a mediator is an encouragement to pay attention to it as one – of many – factors in the struggle for a better society.

Polarisation

The *Oxford English Dictionary* (OED) defines polarisation as 'The accentuation of a difference between two things or groups' (OED Online 2012b). When looking for signs of (de-) polarisation in our four cities, we considered polarisation (as well as attempts at cohesion) as a procedural, relative and contextual phenomenon. It is *procedural* – an accentu*ation* as the above definition indicates – because before reaching a *state* of division, a *process* of polarisation takes place, where different groups start to drift apart. It is *relative* because we should not assume that only one part of the population is departing from an absolute fixed point of normality. Rather, polarisation involves two (or more) poles that increase the *relative* distance from each other. It would therefore be overly simplistic to put all the blame on one section of the population as 'drifting away' from mainstream society. Prejudice, stereotypes, xenophobia, economic patronisation and so on can often be diagnosed among several social groups.

A conclusion of the above is that we have to be careful not to blindly adopt the popular vilification of those portrayed as polarising as necessarily evil. As highlighted by participants of our kick-off workshop emphasised, radicals typically consider themselves as representatives of their people's legitimate causes against oppression. As the etymology of the word indicates, radicals simply try to tackle the root (Latin: *radix*) causes of problems. This position does not make us spineless relativists because we do retain our strong normative position that we categorically reject violent *means* by which some radicals pursue their goals.

STRUCTURE OF THE BOOK

The book is divided into three sections: A conceptual one (chapters 2 and 3), an empirical one (chapters 4 to 7) and a final section on the wider debate in the field (chapters 8, 9 and 10).

Chapter 2 is an overview of the Economic and Social Research Council (ESCR) project 'The urban environment: Mirror and mediator of radicalisation' that undergirds the majority of this book. The project genesis, research questions, case study locations and characteristics, the research executions and outputs (including an exhibition in four languages – still available) are described in this chapter.

Chapter 3 delves into the significance and conceptual foundation and academic remit of the project. This chapter derives from a paper that the authors published in the *Journal of Urban Technology* in 2009 (Fregonese and Brand 2009) as part of a special issue titled 'The Architecture of War and Peace'. It demonstrates the strengths but also the limits of conventional disciplinary perspectives to capture socio-material dynamics within contested cities. It also shows how an approach inspired by Science and Technology Studies (STS) can help overcome some of these blind spots and how it could become a useful and original theoretical platform from which to study the built environment and cities as socio-material phenomena.

Each of the four following empirical chapters deals with one case-study city. Luckily, thanks to the support of the Manchester Architecture Research Centre (MARC), we could illustrate these chapters with a very generous amount of visuals.

Chapter 4 presents the case of Belfast – a city where conflict has been ongoing for decades and has deep historical roots. The chapter analyses Belfast's management of division – through defensive architecture and the so-called 'peace lines' – and the attempts at de-escalation such as the award-winning Stewartstown Road Regeneration Project (SRRP) in the south-west of the city.

Chapter 5 considers the ways past and present conflicts have impacted on Beirut's everyday life through micro- and macro-urban changes, from the reconstruction of the entire city centre to the still widespread presence of politico-confessional territorial markers. Within an ongoing polarisation process involving multiple groups, several spatial interventions can be identified, that aim at promoting interaction or at least conviviality. In Beirut, it seems that not only the counter-voices to sectarianism and violence (both top-down and grassroots), but most importantly their transformation into urban interventions, have the most significant effect and legacy.

Chapter 6 is about Berlin and the polarisation that the growing presence of right-wing extremism has caused in our case-study neighbourhood of Lichtenberg in former East Berlin. Right-wing extremism is mirrored not only in the presence of signs and territorial markers like stickers and graffiti, but also by specific infrastructural hubs. While Crime Prevention Through Environmental Design (CPTED) has been a traditional response in tackling crime related to right-wing extremism as general crime, we found that counter-voices from the civil society – and their material manifestation – play an essential role in tackling this specific type of extremism.

Chapter 7 deals with the socio-material processes around a different type of polarisation taking place in the neighbourhood of Slotervaart in western Amsterdam. Here, we observed the socio-technical dynamics of relative polarisation involving the native Dutch society and the Muslim community in the Netherlands, in the context of recent episodes of Islamic radicalisation that the government is currently tackling.

Inspired by a Charter for Spaces of Positive Encounters that we produced following fieldwork research and a rigorous qualitative analysis of our data using Nvivo software package, Chapter 8 deals with the implications of the project for UK policies. It examines critically the views of the built environment as trigger of suspicion about terrorist activity held by the PREVENT strand of the UK national security strategy and by the UK Metropolitan Police Counter-Terrorism Hotline: . A condensed version of the Charter is also available on the project exhibition website: www.urbanpolarisation.org.

Chapter 9 consists of interviews with four prominent built environment scholars: Scott Bollens, Jon Calame, Frank Gaffikin and Wendy Pullan. These conversations touch upon a number of common themes such as the lack of importance given to the built environment by experts of conflict and by international policy representatives; the knowledge gap between built environment professionals and social scientists who study processes of conflict; the importance of contact and interaction with difference as opposed to 'us versus them' discourses; and the way in which different scales and forms of polarisation and radicalisation enter and modify the everyday life of thousands inhabitants of cities beyond the radicalised groups' ideological realm.

Our co-investigator, Jon Coaffee of the University of Birmingham, kindly wrote the epilogue to the book, in Chapter 10. Jon reflects on the power of materiality to project and influence feelings as well as specific ideologies, which highlights architecture and planning's potential but also responsibility to deal productively with difference in our increasingly multicultural cities. Jon calls for a cultural change among professionals of the built environment and for a better understanding of the importance of planning, urban design and architecture – especially as participatory processes – in tackling polarisation, inequality and other social grievances.

2

The Urban Environment:
Mirror and Mediator of Radicalisation?

THE PROJECT

Each author has personally experienced the everyday reality in a contested city: Ralf Brand grew up in a quiet, relatively untroubled, mid-size town in southern Germany and moved to Belfast, the capital of 'The Troubles', in 2005 for a Lectureship at Queen's University's Institute of Spatial and Environmental Planning.

From 2000, Sara Fregonese has travelled to Beirut numerous times, researching contemporary sovereignty, conflict and urban space for her undergraduate, doctoral and postdoctoral projects (Fregonese 2008, 2009, 2012b, forthcoming).

Ralf was involved in the action research project 'Contested cities – urban universities' (Brand et al. 2008), led by Frank Gaffikin, in which a team of urban planners, political scientists, community activists, designers, conflict resolution specialists and others tried to shape the future of certain neighbourhoods in Belfast towards more amicable relations between nationalist and loyalist residents. During this engagement with the 'swampy lowlands' (Schön 1987: 1) he collected a lot of first-hand experience about the community tensions in Northern Ireland and, given his PhD in Community and Regional Planning, he quickly understood his colleagues' concerns with the spatial and material aspects of the situation. Ralf's conceptual angle of Science and Technology Studies (STS), however, made him also notice the relevance of artefacts that a planner would not typically deal with: The molecular composition of paint, for example, because it determines how easily inflammatory graffities can be removed. The shape to which bushes are trimmed, because low branches make it possible to store various kinds of 'ammunition' for the next riot. He therefore wanted to investigate the role of materiality for conflict along the whole spectrum of things: From city-wide infrastructures and street layouts via building floor plans and landscaping issues all the way to roller shutters, bricks and screws.

The review of the existing literature also revealed a remarkable gap in terms of the *state* of conflict and contestation. Most previous studies and publications dealt with conflict in full swing or at least at a certain static level. Not a whole lot had been written about the role of the urban environment during the *process* of polarisation. In other words, the existing literature had a lot to say about materiality in situations when community relations were bad; but not so much when they were getting worse. Conversely, little had been published about the way in which 'things' could be strategically enrolled in efforts to improve the situation.[1] It was this focus on the *dynamics* of polarisation and de-polarisation that eventually led to the idea of a new research project. Around that time, in June 2006, Ralf moved to the Manchester Architecture Research Centre at the University of Manchester. There he met Jon Coaffee who had led several projects on counter-terrorism and urban resilience. Jon alerted Ralf to the 'New security challenges' funding programme of the Economic and Social Research Council (ESRC), the Arts and Humanities Research Council (AHRC) and the Foreign and Commonwealth Office (FCO). This programme had just issued the call for proposals for its third funding round under the heading '"Radicalisation" and violence – a critical reassessment'. Ralf's application – with Jon as co-investigator – was successful. The award was for £208,000 (full economic costing) and registered under the ESRC Grant Number RES-181-25-0028.

The project started under the title 'The urban environment: Mirror and mediator of radicalisation' on 30 September 2007. Shortly thereafter, Sara Fregonese emerged as the most competent applicant for the position as research associate, not only due to her Arabic skills but also because of her knowledge of the field in general and her PhD research on Beirut in particular. In the morning of 28 February 2008 the first Advisory Council meeting was held in Manchester, attended by Simon Guy (Manchester), Wendy Pullan (Cambridge), Thomas Bürk (Berlin), Frank Gaffikin (Belfast), Maarten Poorter (Amsterdam) and Rachid Chamoun (Beirut). The latter questioned the term *radicalisation* in the project title and pointed out that many groups we are interested in do not perceive themselves as radicals but as advocates of what they perceive as entirely legitimate causes. We therefore gladly adopted his recommendation to add a question mark to the project title. This also resonated well with the inverted commas around the word radicalisation in the full title of the funding programme (see above). They were deliberately introduced to indicate the unclear and contested perception and interpretation of this sensitive term. During the first few months we realised more and more that the term radicalisation always implies the movement and withdrawal of one group away from some speaker's apparent normal, accepted or standard position. It is therefore inevitably a judgemental term. *Polarisation*, however, seems to be more neutral because it describes a more relative phenomenon which does not pre-answer the question which one of two (or more) poles moves away from the other. For all conceptual and programmatic purposes we therefore eventually settled for the project title 'The urban environment: Mirror and mediator of polarisation?'

The 'New security challenges' programme had previously been criticised for its perceived Islamophobic undertones. In fact, a group of scientists from all over the UK boycotted the scheme. In response, the original call for proposals for the

---

1   For a more detailed analysis of the existing literature see Chapter 3.

Map 2.1
Case study
locations

third funding round was withdrawn, rewritten and then released in a much more carefully worded version. We went to great length to avoid similar allegations and therefore devised a sampling rationale that deliberately contrasts and compares different types of radicalisation or polarisation while not shying away from issues around Islamic fundamentalism. Mainly practical considerations related to funding and time made us decide that the manageable number of case studies was going to be four. With four cases a strategic set of symmetries could be investigated and contrasted. Case study contenders included Samarkand, Beirut, Mostar, Kuala Lumpur, Fribourg, Brussels, Belfast, Paris, Amsterdam, Montreal, Sarajevo and Berlin. In the latter case the tension under study would not have been the Cold War era conflict between East and West but the recent surge in right-wing extremism. After several rounds of constellation-testing we settled for the four cases shown in Map 2.1 and mentioned in Table 2.1.

Table 2.1 Case study characteristics 1

		Belfast	Berlin	Beirut	Amsterdam
Islamic dimension	Yes			X	X
	No	X	X		
Severity	(Formerly) civil-war character	X		X	
	Individual incidents		X		X

Given the inevitably binary nature of tables, that is, their inherent inability to capture nuances, we would like to encourage readers to take these classifications with a grain of salt or, in academic speech, as heuristic tools only that at least allowed us to sample our cases transparently, strategically and justifiably.

As alluded to before, the juxtaposition of Beirut and Amsterdam to two other cities reflects the purpose of the 'New security challenges' programme to study '"radicalisation" and violence purportedly in the name of Islam' (Economic and Social Research Council 2007: 1) but not at the risk of leaving blind spots about other attention-worthy forms of social polarisation, especially not if information derived from the latter can help us to better understand the former. We also deliberately wanted to study the situation in 'classic' conflict cities and compare it to the one in, shall we say, cities characterised by 'milder' forms of tensions – obviously without wanting to belittle the physical and emotional pain experienced by their victims. Further details about all the four cases are provided in Chapters 4 to 7. At this point, however, it seems necessary to present at least a few of their basic characteristics in Table 2.2.

Table 2.2 Case study characteristics 2

	Belfast	Berlin	Beirut	Amsterdam
Perceived radical groups	Nationalist and loyalist extremists	Neo-Nazis	Hezbollah and other political and sectarian groups	Young people with immigration background – also native Dutch
Historical roots	Centuries	Several decades	Contested time-scales; from millennia to post-2005	Post-colonial
Recent developments	Signs of rapprochement	Professionalisation	Stop-and-go conflict	(Counter-) radicalisation
Qualities of contest	Religious, political, linguistic	Political, ethnic	Religious, political	Religious, cultural

Of importance is also the fact that all of these cities are, without exception, subject to the very same trends. Processes of gentrification, for example, are in full swing in Beirut as well as in Berlin, in Amsterdam and equally in Belfast. Similarly, all four cities experience the unyielding forces of global capital. They are all concerned about their reputation in the international tourism market. At the same time, they are all under the influence of external state and non-state actors, ranging from the European Union, to the Syrian ruler family and the Irish Diaspora in the United States. These combinations of similarities and differences were not only the intellectual spine of our sampling and analysis strategy. As attested by explicit feedback from the attendees of our stakeholder workshops the exploration of shared and contrasting experiences was also the most valued aspect of these events.

We included stakeholder workshops as a deliberate element into our empirical programme because we were convinced that the presence of a 'strategic sample of all beneficiaries   will help to maximise the relevance of the research to their needs and interests by co-determining its foci' as we argued in the original funding application. In essence, we wanted to make sure that we do not only pursue research questions of pure academic value in ivory tower mode. We were keen to produce something of relevance for practitioners in the 'swampy lowlands' – not simply by disseminating our findings to them as passive receivers at the end of the project but by giving them a say in the shaping of the research questions at the outset of the project. The first workshop, held on 28–29 February, was attended by the members of our Advisory Council, team members, support staff, PhD students plus 14 representatives from our case-study cities. From Amsterdam: Lucas Evers, Dennis Kaspori, Jan Simons and Eric Van der Kooij. From Beirut: Antoine Mansour and Robert Saliba. From Belfast: John Hoey, Andy Kennedy, Louise McNeill and Chris O'Halloran. From Berlin: Claudia Luzar, Claudia Schmid and Björn Von Swieykowski.

RESEARCH QUESTIONS

With the benefit of these experts' input, we then fine-tuned the analytical parameters for the ensuing fieldwork phase, cast into the following set of research questions:

Research Question 1

How does polarisation become materially imprinted in cities characterised by different patterns of conflict and polarisation? This question tackles not only the outcomes of polarisation but also the conditions under which it operates. It is likely that different types of polarisation at different stages prefer different visible and tangible manifestations of their work. For example, the purpose of nurturing a financial and electoral support base seems to require the physical display of strength. The preparation of clandestine missions, however, might require a deliberate degree of unobtrusiveness.[2]

Research Question 2

Are certain design features of cities (buildings, infrastructures, public spaces, etc.) particularly conducive to the generation and acceleration of different forms of polarisation? This research question addresses the mediating function of the urban environment. It guided our critical assessment of the diverse causes of polarisation

---

2   The 'Hamburg Cell', the base of several of the 9/11 pilots, was located in an almost bourgeois quarter of Hamburg.

whereby the understanding of causes was even widened to encompass stabilising, enabling, accelerating and potentially alleviating factors. This question was also designed to contribute to the 'Prevent strand' of the UK's Counter Terrorism policy which aims to 'chang[e] the environment in which the extremists and those radicalising others can operate' (HM Government 2006: 1) – this obviously requires detailed knowledge about these environments, understood in a quite literal sense.

Research Question 3

Is it possible to steer the momentum of co-evolution between social conditions and the urban environment to facilitate friendly encounters between groups that would otherwise diverge? This question explores how the conditions analysed in RQ1 and RQ2 could be otherwise. We thought that if this question can be answered affirmatively, it would provide justification for hope. Hope, not in the sense that polarisation can be extirpated simply by means of clever interventions in the built environment. But it would provide arguments for concrete local actions to facilitate friendly encounters and, ideally, to help channel dissatisfaction into non-violent forms of expression. Subject to the caveats about transferability (see below) it would provide encouragement and advice to agencies and non-governmental organisations in cities in the UK[3] and elsewhere.

Research Question 4

How transferable are the findings between and beyond the four case studies? If we were to avoid over-generalisation it had to be of utmost importance to resist the temptation of best practice 'fixes' – especially in the case of contested cities that are, by their very nature, characterised by historically and culturally specific factors. We therefore critically assessed the degree of context specificity of our empirical research findings, carefully searched for patterns of social-technical constellations and, wherever applicable, highlighted generalisable findings.

EXECUTION

The above decisions determined a good degree of our empirical programme and thus allowed us to apply for ethics approval from the University of Manchester's Research Ethics Committee. Given the highly sensitive nature of our subject this procedure required utmost care and led to very helpful exchanges with members of said committee. The same is true with regards to the risk assessment which we had to conduct in order to obtain fieldwork approval from our institutional unit,

---

3   Potential cities include Bradford, Oldham, Burnley and 'Rochdale, Preston, Bolton, Huddersfield, Tower Hamlets in east London, Ilford/Barking, Camden in north London, Nottingham and Leeds' which Gurbux Singh, then head of the Commission for Racial Equality, mentioned to the British government as 'potential hotspots … with visibly segregated housing and schools' (Travis 2006).

the School of Environment and Development. The importance of this step was underlined by the incidents in Beirut in mid-2008 which made us postpone our fieldwork in Lebanon for a while. Back then, tensions between government and opposition militant factions exploded in deadly armed clashes in the streets of Beirut and other Lebanese cities, followed by several weeks of instability before a national agreement was reached. The complete empirical programme consisted of the following fieldwork periods:

Belfast:	23 June – 3 July 2008	18 interviews
Berlin:	1–12 September 2008	23 interviews
Amsterdam:	27 October – 8 November 2008	31 interviews
Beirut:	26 January – 5 February 2009	18 interviews

With two team members on each trip, a total of 92 person-days were spent in situ. This allowed us to conduct semi-structured interviews with 90 individuals, including local politicians, planners, academics, community activists, NGO representatives, architects, shopkeepers, company managers, city councillors, victim organisations, artists, police officers and so-called extremists. Given the benefit of our previous research in Belfast (Ralf) and Beirut (Sara) and given our in-depth conversations with all members of the advisory council we had the privilege of listening to the views, opinions, sometimes even traumas and secrets, of almost 150 individuals to which we would like to extend our sincere gratitude. Where we refer to individuals in our findings we always used pseudonyms – unless instructed otherwise by individual interviewees. The long list of participants also includes the attendees at our second stakeholder workshop on 21–22 May 2009, which was designed to check the validity of our city-specific as well as our cross-city findings and to discuss suggested policy implications. The following individuals attended this workshop in addition to several of those already mentioned above: Youssef Chaitani, Amira Solh (Beirut), Carl Chung, Michael Mallé, Heike Marquardt (Berlin), Sylvia Gordon, Liam O'Dowd, Ken Sterrett (Belfast), Atef Hamdy, Colin Mellis, Thijl Sunier, Nanke Verloo and Tobias Woldendorp (Amsterdam).

OUTPUTS

We presented our findings at various conferences and workshops to academics and practitioners in Germany, Lebanon, the Netherlands, several cities in the UK, Italy, Bulgaria and even Qatar. Our conclusions were also published in a number of peer-reviewed journal articles (Brand 2009b, 2009c, 2011; Fregonese and Brand 2009). Maybe most noteworthy as an output from an academic project is our touring exhibition. Two Austrian artists, Wolfgang Obermair and Andrea Börner, enthusiastically tackled the task of translating our findings into such a medium for wider public consumption. They managed to create a visually appealing, spatially flexible, lightweight, interactive, easy to assemble product (see Figure 2.1) which was unveiled at THE PLACE in Belfast on 5 November 2009.

Figure 2.1
Project exhibition
in Beirut

According to the gallery manager, this event was the best attended one in all of 2009. The exhibition in one of its four languages (English, German, Dutch, Arabic) continued its tour throughout 2010 to Beirut (1–16 April), Manchester (10–22 April and 25 June – 3 July), Berlin (22–28 May) and Amsterdam (12 June – 28 August) as planned in the original bid. In addition, it was displayed upon specific requests at the Royal United Services Institute (RUSI) in London, the University of Exeter and Royal Holloway University of London. The exhibition was part of a package of project-related outputs which was nominated in 2010 for the RIBA President's Award for Research in the category Outstanding University-located Research. It made it into the final round of three remaining contenders but eventually was trumped by Ralf's colleague's submission – congratulations Albena![4]

A short video about this project and further visual material about the project exhibition is available at www.youtube.com/user/brandrg/videos. The exhibition per se is still available free of charge from the authors. Lastly, after reviewing the end-of-project report and the project's impact report (both are available on the ESRC website) the ESRC evaluated the project as 'very good'.

---

4   Albena Yaneva's study 'An Ethnography of Architecture'.

3

Polarisation as a Socio-Material Phenomenon: A Bibliographical Review[1]

Belfast, the capital of Northern Ireland, has suffered for many decades from a conflict between Protestant (Loyalist/Unionist) and Catholic (Nationalist/Republican) communities about identity, national belonging and political representation. The bombing campaigns, arson attacks and other atrocities sparked by these tensions killed 1,600 people and forced thousands of families to relocate to more and more homogeneous ethnic neighbourhoods. Over the last 10 years, significant progress towards a more peaceful society has been made, but the problems are still deep-seated.

The Westlink motorway runs through Belfast and separates, along several stretches, a number of Protestant and Catholic neighbourhoods where it acts, by implication, as an 'interface' between these antagonistic groups. Many stones and other missiles have, therefore, crossed the Westlink on their way to hurt, intimidate and annoy residents on 'the other' side. Political rapprochement, heroic efforts of community workers, combined with various material interventions like fences and walls, reduced the number of attacks to a bearable level over recent years until, in late 2007, serious sectarian violence erupted again in one particular location.

Residences on both sides of the motorway were pelted with stones at such a frequency that residents began to protect the windows of their houses and the windshields of their cars with bars and plywood. Heather Elwood from the Village Focus Group reported that 72 incidents took place in only three weeks in 2007, whereas in previous years only occasional problems had occurred and careful reconciliation work had been under way (Northern Ireland News 2007). The fast deterioration of the situation left the Northern Ireland Office (NIO) no alternative

1   From Sara Fregonese and Ralf Brand (2009) 'Polarization as a socio-material phenomenon: A bibliographical review', *Journal of Urban Technology*, 16(2), 9–33, http://dx.doi.org/10.1080/10630730903278546. Copyright © The Society of Urban Technology, reprinted by permission of Taylor & Francis Ltd (www.tandfonline.com) on behalf of The Society of Urban Technology.

Figure 3.1 The completed bridge from the north side of the Westlink. The Protestant area lies behind the trees at the left and the Catholic area is at the right. The new 'peace line' fence protecting the latter can clearly be seen.

but to construct a 10-metre high anti-ballistic fence to protect a row of houses (Interview with NIO representative, 27 June 2008).

Typically, one attempting to understand this escalation would enquire whether the political situation in Northern Ireland deteriorated that autumn, or whether an aggressive speech rekindled cross-community hatred. However, in the Westlink case, the answer lies somewhere else and in something more mundane and concrete than political discourse: It was the construction of a footbridge across the Westlink.

Earlier in 2007, construction began on a pedestrian bridge connecting the two sides of the Westlink as part of a major upgrade of this motorway (Figure 3.1 and see http://tinyurl.com/953p2kp). The bridge was mainly meant to facilitate the pedestrian connection between the Royal Victoria Hospital, located in a Catholic area, and the predominantly Protestant Donegal Road neighbourhood and further parts of Belfast. The legal requirement of a wheelchair ramp resulted in the bridge being moved 40 metres from its originally planned location to its final position right in front of several houses. However, after this move, the bridge turned into 'a magnet for youngsters because it is so easy for them to access the other side' (Northern Ireland News 2007), according to Daniel Jack from the Safer Neighbourhood Project. Other community workers argued that the 'design and location of the bridge gives youths an easy escape route' (Northern Ireland News 2007) and thus makes the risk of an attack on enemy turf more calculable. Wheelchair access on the northern bridgehead was placed on a gradually sloping mound, which created the perfect elevation of a launching spot for missile attacks (see Figure 3.1). Elwood complained that 'There was no consultation with either community about the location. If there had been, we could have told them this sort of thing would happen' (Northern Ireland News 2007).

This example demonstrates that the actions of human beings cannot appropriately be understood without considering their physical surroundings. Architect Kim Dovey (1999) argues that 'everyday life "takes place"', and it seems a logical extension of this observation that attacks, polarisation, community tensions and even radicalisation also 'take place'. Conversely, the Westlink Bridge emphasises

the importance of understanding the social processes that influence the location, shape and material qualities of artefacts. In short, humans and non-humans have agency and neither deserves primacy. The material and the social are inseparable parts of a recursive 'socio-material loop' in which they continuously affect each other in hugely complex and often unpredictable ways. To look at only the social or the material element of this dynamic would be like watching only one half of a tennis game as Latour (1992) puts it. In this chapter, we examine how existing literature[2] across a range of disciplines manages or fails to grasp such bi-directional processes between social conditions and material settings in community cohesion, (de-)polarisation and even radicalisation.

In the first section, we explore literature focusing on the urban aspects of war and post-war situations. These contributions bring together an interdisciplinary pool of scholars, including social scientists as well as architects and planners. However, they mostly focus on the deplorable state of war but tend to overlook the processes of escalation towards it.

In the second section, we review studies that do consider the procedural aspects of polarisation and radicalisation. However, we notice that they tend to treat them as purely socio-cultural and psychological phenomena. It appears that they would benefit from complementary attention to non-human agency.

Conversely, the third section focuses on literature from disciplines with an inherent emphasis on materiality such as architecture, planning and environmental criminology. Some of their representatives seem, however, to display a belief in 'material fixes' to the extent that they underestimate human agency.

Lastly, we assess the value of Science and Technology Studies (STS) as a conceptual framework to holistically grasp the phenomena in question. Although STS seems to escape a number of problems we identified in other disciplines, it suffers from a disregard for substantive issues at the intersection of the urban environment and community relations. This myopia, however, appears remediable. Consequently, STS emerges as a conceptual platform that could contribute to more comprehensive understandings of the socio-material worlds through which polarisation 'takes place'.

---

2   The clustering rationale we apply to the existing literature is of our own choosing as a means to achieve a manageable overview of the arguments on polarisation.

WAR CITY LITERATURE: MORE PROCESSES, PLEASE!

This section reviews some of the literature on the socio-material nature of urban conflict, that is, the ways in which war shapes urban infrastructure and how urban infrastructure affects the course of war. We are interested in this strand of literature because it neither treats conflict exclusively as a mental or (geo)political issue, nor does it portray the urban environment as the determinant force of war. However, we also think that these arguments would benefit from more attention to the processes whereby societies become polarised (or are in the course of reconciliation) rather than focusing only on the state of open violence.

A large number of scholars in architecture and planning embrace the notion that the processes and results of urban development are shaped by and shape socio-political conditions. Planning as a socio-political practice is increasingly seen not as 'an innocent, value-neutral activity [but as] deeply political' (Healey 1997). Translated into a context of urban conflict, Wendy Pullan[3] raises similar arguments for the case of Jerusalem where urban infrastructure and politics are tightly intertwined. Here, even 'the highways are political' (Pullan et al. 2007: 177). From another perspective, urban infrastructure can become a tool of resistance in a highly contested space when through 'market stalls, tea stands [and] paratransport' (Pullan et al. 2007: 193) the relationships constituting the Palestinian social fabric are reclaimed. Oren Yiftachel (1998) is also among this group of scholars who scrutinise architecture and planning for their political and geopolitical agendas including ethnic domination, military tactics and other 'dark sides'. More recently, Calame and Charlesworth (2009) highlighted the role of architecture and design in war-ravaged cities by analysing a number of 'divided cities' in which they explore the parallels between the physical evolution of their hard inner boundaries (walls, dividing lines, and so on) and the social conditions that physical separations effect.

Some authors who write about the damage inflicted upon the physical fabric of cities call for a non-anthropocentric approach that describes attacks against the urban built fabric as 'urbicide' (Coward 2006). The negative implications of these acts for the well-being of human communities are the foundation upon which arguments rest to pursue architectural damage in the international justice system (Bevan 2005). Cultural and physical representations of Western and 'Oriental' (especially Arab) cities have been employed to reinforce discourses of security, defence (for the cities in the 'West') or danger and attack (against those in the 'East') by the advocates of the 'War on Terror'. Such arguments are the focus of Urban Geopolitics, a body of literature about the relations between the fabric of cities and acts of political violence (Graham 2001, 2004, 2006). Urban Geopolitics stems from the need to critically analyse the city as 'both target and arena of war' (Coward 2007) in the light of a so-called repositioning of conflicts in the post-Cold War era, from 'the open countryside of western Europe' (Coward 2007) into urban terrains. This repositioning has been advocated by post-1989 military theory considering cities as the ultimate terrains of the so-called 'new wars' of the twenty-first century (Kaldor 1999; Peters 1996; Press 1999). These strategies conceive urban

3   Conflict in Cities project, www.arct.cam.ac.uk/conflictincities.

environments as flexible terrains that can be entirely reworked for military control and security purposes (Weizman 2004).

While there is a remarkable number of studies about the material aspects of cities at war that investigate the role of architecture and planning in a state of open violence (Bogdanovic 1994; Coward 2002, 2004, 2006; Lindqvist 2002; Mostar Architects Association 1993; Ramadan 2009), relatively few scholars tackle the process of (de-)escalation towards or away from violence. In other words, the existing literature on the mutually shaping relationship between the material and social in conditions of open violence would benefit from more complementary studies on the socio-material processes before and after violence erupts. Architect Esther Charlesworth affirms that 'more research is needed to observe the patterns that lead to civil violence and displacement and to look at how this is manifested in the physical domain'.

Some scholars have contextualised non-violent (but escalating) issues of ethnic identity (Roseman et al. 1996), segregation, racism, inclusion and exclusion, territoriality and discourses of defence (Gold and Revill 2000) within conceptualisations of urban space (Keith 2005). Among the arguments which are attentive to the built and architectural aspects of polarisation of communities are those dealing with the production and reproduction of inequality through mundane planning and infrastructure laws and the limitation of civic freedoms brought by ubiquitous surveillance technologies (Coaffee 2003; Gold and Revill 2000; Weizman 2007).

Besides acknowledging the need for more study of polarisation processes, Charlesworth also calls for more synergy between political actors, social scientists and spatial experts in understanding de-polarisation in war-torn cities. She argues that 'achieving political and ethnic collaboration … requires architects to consult with non-spatial professionals such as politicians, environmentalists, sociologists, psychiatrists, economists, and community representatives' (Charlesworth 2006: 132) Also Scott Bollens (1998a, 1998b, 1999, 2002, 2006) is an influential exponent of research on the impact that both urban policy and urban design can have for post-war de-escalation in conflict-ridden cities. Here, social reconstruction becomes inextricably linked to physical reconstruction. Likewise, the material fabric of the city acquires particular importance because it constitutes the basis for the future reconciled city: 'Everything from sewage systems and road networks to markets, and playgrounds, and river promenades. [In such situations] the planning process can help build trust and understanding across communities, reshaping not only the physical but the social and political geography of the city' (Evans 2006: xii).

In this sense, Charlesworth argues, 'post-war urban planning can be a peace-building process in itself' (Evans 2006: xi) and it has the power of stirring positive dynamics between communities and architecture. Moreover, she stresses the possibility of a spatial thinking and practice that can prevent processes of societal division, and enquiries whether it is 'possible to design clever buffers, remedies, or release valves in order to mitigate the worst effects of the negative [social] changes, assuming we cannot stop them altogether?' (Charlesworth 2006: 132).

Despite the growing acknowledgement of the political value of planning processes and outcomes, these need to be considered more carefully. As Charlesworth notes, 'there has been little comparative research informing design professionals about effective examples of using architecture as a peace-building tool' (Charlesworth 2006: 15). Patsy Healey also affirms the valuable role of planning to promote social co-existence by forging synergies with policy sectors that are normally not involved with planning, architecture and urban design. She highlights the importance of understanding 'social polarization [as] … an active, ongoing process of socio-spatial differentiation' (Healey 1997: 122). This argument is similar to Watson's encouragement to pay attention to spaces in which 'people rub along, or don't' and the spaces which accompany 'the conditions under which violent and negative emotions can erupt' (Watson 2006: 2). In a nutshell, it seems possible and worthwhile to complement the considerable body of literature on the socio-material nature of open violence with a more systematic focus on the processes that precede and follow a state of conflict. In the next section, we will review studies that do consider these processes, but pay very little attention to their material dimension.

SOCIO-POLITICAL LITERATURE: MORE MATTER, PLEASE!

Studies centred on processes of escalation, polarisation and even radicalisation come from different disciplinary angles. From a database search of over 77 studies on radicalisation from 1977 to 2008 (see Figure 3.2), it emerges that research on this issue is strongly concentrated within the political, sociological and psychological-behavioural sciences. From these perspectives, the problem is usually framed in ways that demand a focus on 'the psychological process across all levels of terrorist involvement' (Horgan 2008), individual and group identity formation, social networks and the role of ideological orthodoxy (McCauley and Moskalenko 2008). A remarkable number of studies in this area concern counter-terrorism strategies and the psychological mechanisms of radicalisation in individuals. In other words, these studies identify discourses, beliefs and mindsets as the realms where answers to radicalisation can be found and emphasise the importance of (geo)political grievances, counter-arguments, education, change of perception and 'positive' role models (Kirby 2007; Ryan 2007; Sageman 2008; Weiman and Von Knop 2008).

In this cohort of studies, the socio-political and psychological aspects are rarely or almost never complemented by analyses or descriptions of the material settings where radicalisation takes place. In other words, the social goes without the material. An attempt to understand the deterioration of community relations across the Westlink in Belfast from this perspective would miss some crucial explanatory variables. This is not to say, of course, that the pedestrian bridge is responsible for these skirmishes, but that it doubtlessly facilitates the acting-out of a certain mental state.

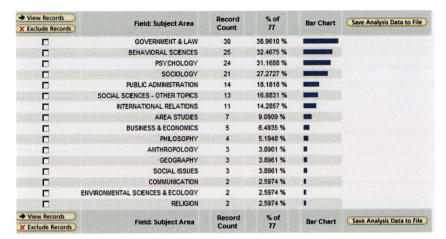

View Records / Exclude Records	Field: Subject Area	Record Count	% of 77	Bar Chart	Save Analysis Data to File
☐	GOVERNMENT & LAW	30	38.9610 %		
☐	BEHAVIORAL SCIENCES	25	32.4675 %		
☐	PSYCHOLOGY	24	31.1688 %		
☐	SOCIOLOGY	21	27.2727 %		
☐	PUBLIC ADMINISTRATION	14	18.1818 %		
☐	SOCIAL SCIENCES - OTHER TOPICS	13	16.8831 %		
☐	INTERNATIONAL RELATIONS	11	14.2857 %		
☐	AREA STUDIES	7	9.0909 %		
☐	BUSINESS & ECONOMICS	5	6.4935 %		
☐	PHILOSOPHY	4	5.1948 %		
☐	ANTHROPOLOGY	3	3.8961 %		
☐	GEOGRAPHY	3	3.8961 %		
☐	SOCIAL ISSUES	3	3.8961 %		
☐	COMMUNICATION	2	2.5974 %		
☐	ENVIRONMENTAL SCIENCES & ECOLOGY	2	2.5974 %		
☐	RELIGION	2	2.5974 %		
View Records / Exclude Records	Field: Subject Area	Record Count	% of 77	Bar Chart	Save Analysis Data to File

Figure 3.2 Disciplinary distribution of research on radicalisation between 1970 and 2009

Scholars do occasionally acknowledge the importance of material contexts for polarisation or radicalisation, but they mostly focus on sponsoring and financing support for extremists. Weinberg and Pedahzur (2003) argue that radicalism can be related to a state's economic situation. For example, in countries with poor economies extremist networks can thrive by channelling local socio-economic grievances and thus 'transform themselves into mass-movements' (2003: 7).

The biggest focus of this strand of literature seems to be behaviour, together with ideological predispositions such as universalism, millennialism and Manichean worldviews. These philosophical visions and behavioural attitudes seem to outdo the role of the physical environment that is often depicted as a given. Although some scholars mention spatial segregation as a potential issue, it hardly ever features as a noteworthy variable: 'Whether or not they separate themselves physically from the surrounding community by living in enclaves, for example, fundamentalists typically separate themselves from those around them by their behavior' (Weinberg and Pedahzur 2004: 41–2).

It seems, then, that approaches focusing on radicalisation as an issue of 'extreme' mindsets, beliefs, feelings, ideology and identity might benefit from some kind of 'material turn' or at least from complementary studies about concrete contexts. This argument is not intended to undermine the huge importance and value of these approaches, but it indicates the risk of falling for the allure of social or mental 'fixes' with little spatial and material grounding. There are a number of exceptions to this interpretative strand. A range of studies in community planning and urban design deals with the dynamics of segregation, school design and location and the spatial translations of current ideas about cohesion (Clapper 2006; Ganapati 2008).

Political science scholars have mentioned issues other than mindset in their analyses of radicalisation. Githens-Mazer and O'Duffy highlight the shortcomings of exclusively macro- or micro-level perspectives on radicalisation and argue that macro-level grievances (foreign policy, perceptions of global injustice, etc.) need to be considered together with micro-level conflicts (socio-economic conditions and social networks). Some studies only seek causes of radicalisation within the micro social-psychological mechanisms of 'young and impressionable … ignorant and immature [people] … from a poor background and a broken family' (Githens-Mazer 2008: 21). However, an exclusive focus on the micro-level of social networks of recruitment overlooks the wider grievances weighing on the radicalised individual or group, as O'Duffy (2008) argues. Similarly, analyses relying exclusively on the macro-level highlight the negative impacts of Western foreign policy on domestic radicalisation, but do not follow these impacts on micro-practices such as recruitment and activism. Instead, we need to acknowledge the particular urban and technological dimensions of radicalisation through 'nuanced and well-informed strategic thinking about locating sites where radicalization may be taking place … and how such locations … lead to both ideological and tactical capacities' (Githens-Mazer 2008: 23).

In his work on the links between segregation and Muslim radicalisation, Daniel Varady (2008) points out that we need to research and establish specific links between the presence of extremist behaviours and the presence of a segregated community. Varady argues that this could be made by considering the concrete practices and immediate surroundings of the radicalised subjects, rather than only engaging with abstract issues of identity formation and indoctrination. He argues that 'what is absent from the current debate is any serious analysis of how Muslim population concentrations may help or hurt an immigrant's integration into the broader social fabric' (Varady 2008: 44). The small number of studies on the interactions between segregation and polarisation might explain the 'little evidence of the importance of enclavization vis a vis other factors (e.g., hate speeches by fundamentalist clerics) in contributing to societal instability through rioting or recruitment into terrorist cells' (Varady 2008: 45). We suggest that this evidence could be provided using approaches that combine social aspects such as ideology, role models and so on, with spatial and material aspects that might also have a role to play in polarising communities.

Of course, not the entire gamut of the social sciences suffers from an underexposure of material contexts. Even if not specifically within the theme of polarisation, a range of authors went beyond mainstream constructivist and discursive approaches and called for a more serious consideration of mundane material objects, together with social relations, as mediators of behaviour. Such contributions to the study of material culture and to the understanding of how 'things other than humans make a difference in the way social relations unfold' (Bakker and Bridge 2006: 17–18) have populated the social sciences and especially human geography in the last decade (Jackson 2000). Located 'at the cutting edge of geographical research that seeks to link the material and the immaterial' (Lees 2002: 109) this literature extends the idea of agency from subjects to include objects and their mediating impact on human practices. However, it also highlights the ethical implications of attributing agency to materiality. As Bakker and Bridge warn, 'the resurgence of the material after a decade of social constructionism … should be a reason for pause, since it raises specters of worn-out dualisms, resurgent physicalisms, object fetishism, and environmental determinism' (2006: 8). In the next section, we will turn our attention to some of these aspects.

BUILT ENVIRONMENT LITERATURE: MORE CONTEST, PLEASE!

One of the most problematic aspects of dealing with the material contextuality of social practices is its potential ontological proximity to determinism and its smell of behaviourism, social engineering and manipulation. A considerable body of literature from the 1960s and 1970s employs such assumptions in its claim about the direct impact of the design and management of urban space on crime, anti-social behaviour, or social decay and fragmentation. Derived from this premise is the conclusion that planners and architects can 'design out' certain social problems (Angel 1968; Heimsath 1977; Jeffery 1971; Newman 1972; Wood 1961).

One particular strand within this literature enjoyed an impressive career since the 1970s under the heading 'Environmental Criminology' or as 'Crime Prevention Through Environmental Design' (CPTED). Its basic assumption is that 'an architect, armed with some understanding of the structure of criminal encounter, can simply avoid providing the space which supports it' (Newman 1972: 14). CPTED, therefore, relies on the existence of a causal relation proceeding unilaterally from the physical to the social and nurtures the expectation that social problems can be alleviated, if not solved, by clever physical interventions. However, more nuanced views about the impact of the material on the social co-exist with Newman's. Jane Jacobs' (1961) arguments, for example, although displaying traits of determinism, did not advocate universally applicable material fixes to crime. Jacobs adopted a network-like approach rather than seeking generalised formulas to cure social ills.

In the 1980s, scholars developed approaches to materiality that were still well aware of its impact on undesired social practices, but that nevertheless conceded less room to determinism and adopted a more cautious language. Various disciplines used the idea of 'territoriality' to analyse arrangements of the urban space that discourage, rather than simply prevent, crime and encourage the defensiveness of homes by shaping perceptions of belonging and presence (Brown 1987). Increasingly through the 1980s and 1990s, the cultural turn in the social sciences favoured visions of materiality shaped by sociality rather than the opposite, and the social sciences have reacted cautiously to the deterministic positions of much of the 1970s literature on defensible space.

Recently, deterministic positions seem to be enjoying a certain renaissance in the guise of the ambition that 'the future is a design problem' (Murphy 2004: 79). UK Security Minister, Alan West, seems to have embraced such a vision as evidenced in his recent call to 'design-out' terrorism (Lazell 2009). This and similar approaches, however, have attracted criticism also in the past, when literature on urban change and global security analysed the socially shaped nature and non-neutrality of anti-terrorism measures in urban environments (Coaffee 2003, 2004; Graham 2004).

In our view, the argument that certain design features *automatically* trigger or prevent certain behavioural responses falls short of explaining reality (Hunter

2008). Otherwise, we should expect that every pedestrian crossing the new bridge in Belfast – or anywhere else if the exact same bridge were built in an absolutely identical physical setting – would throw a stone. The vast majority of people, however, do not even feel the urge to do so. The free will and agency of human beings clearly have a role to play. To ignore or underestimate them would imply a belief in 'material fixes', which were debunked as wishful thinking a long time ago. The behaviour of stone-throwing individuals in Belfast has to be understood not as a result of the bridge alone but also of Northern Ireland's history, the individuals' socio-economic condition and previous experience, the macro-political climate and a myriad of other factors. In other words, artefacts do have some kind of agency, but this is just one of thousands in a messy vector-field of teeming agencies.

Shaftoe (2008) acknowledges this by emphasising the importance of socio-economic and political contexts within which he places his recommendations to create 'convivial spaces'. He argues not only for physical interventions that discourage undesirable behaviours but also for those that might facilitate desirable ones. Ultimately, however, he concludes with a list of dos and don'ts that make his rhetorical appreciation of context forgotten and slips back towards the allure of material fixes. In addition, his argument lacks an acknowledgement of how difficult it often is to overcome the obduracy of the existing urban fabric – even if his recommendations were perfectly adapted to local contexts.

But overall, there is clearly a trend among recent contributions to highlight the relational and context-specific nature of sociality and materiality and to consider neither of them as independent (Bakker and Bridge 2006). In other words, the material is not seen as determinant of the social, but as mediator in a relation with the social. Consequently, the image of the architect and planner has also shifted from 'spatial hero' with ready fixes for social problems to one spatial actor among many (Miessen and Basar 2004).

Healey, therefore, argues that planning 'is an activity conducted by, and in relation to, specific people concerned about specific places. How it works out is contingent upon the particular history and geography of these places' (1997: 86).

It seems evident that a more nuanced view of the relationship between the material and the social than the dominant deterministic one of the 1970s is emerging also in reflections on social, ethnic and political tensions and violence. Shifting away from abstract theorisations of violence, Thrift defines it as 'an expanding series of practices in which objects … have a more than incidental place' (Thrift 2007: 277) blurring the ontological boundaries between the human and non-human elements of the lived reality of violence.

In the next section, we will assess whether or not Science and Technology Studies (STS) might be an appropriate conceptual framework for investigating social (de-)polarisation. This assumption is based on the claims about the field of STS being good at understanding how humans and non-humans jointly compose reality.

THE SCIENCE AND TECHNOLOGY STUDIES APPROACH:
MORE TOPICS PLEASE!

Some scholars, including the authors, are experimenting with an alternative conceptual frame through which the phenomena of polarisation and radicalisation and their embeddedness in the material world may be viewed. It is inspired by the research tradition of Science and Technology Studies (STS), which originated in sociological studies of science that tried to understand how scientific results are socially shaped. Since its inception during the 1960s, STS has had the project of presenting an understandable vision of the whole process of technological innovation as a non-linear relationship between invention, development, dissemination and appropriation. Although STS is not a monolithic school of thought, most of its exponents share the conviction that a Cartesian split between subject and object, matter and mind, technologies and humans or, in our context, the built environment and societies, is misleading. Rather, these pairs must be treated as emergent and mutually constituting. A strand within STS called Actor-Network Theory (ANT) takes this notion furthest and endorses a radical ontological 'symmetry' between humans and non-humans whereby both have agency, act upon and respond to the other (Latour 2005). The corollary of this position is that a distinction between something social and something material operates with false ontological categories, that such a distinction imposes neat categories where no neat categories exist and, consequentially, that the boundary between humans and non-humans is blurry if not undistinguishable.

   In the wake of such an acknowledgement comes the necessity to escape the ontological trap implied in commonsensical words like 'social' or 'material'. Many STS scholars, therefore, have proposed new words and new meanings for existing words such as assemblages, cosmos, actants, translation, delegation, or quasi-objects to circumnavigate these semantic cliffs. The same purpose motivated Donna Haraway (1991) to introduce the idea of cyborgs as an ontological category of our partly human, partly non-human existence. In a similar move, Latour exemplifies the relationship between technologies and human beings with the notion of a 'gun-person' (Latour 1993), that is a genuinely new entity that emerges when a gun and a human being get together and form a new association. For Latour, it is not guns that kill nor people that kill; the culprit is the combination of a gun with a person:

> The dual mistake of the materialists and of the sociologists is to start with essences, either those of subjects or those of objects ... Either you give too much to the gun or too much to the gun-holder. Neither the subject, nor the object, nor their goals are fixed for ever. We have to shift our attention to this unknown X, this hybrid which can truly be said to act. (Latour 1993: 6)

Meanwhile, back at the Westlink in Belfast, a new entity has emerged: The 'bridge-person'. In fact, we would argue that neither the bridge in itself nor the engineering company that designed and built it bear the full blame for the outbreak of some skirmishes since late 2007. Conversely, it would be an oversimplification to dump the entire responsibility onto the stone-throwers, because the poorly thought-through location and design of the new bridge have also contributed to encouraging the behaviour of stone-throwing by making it materially easier. In cities with polarisation and radicalisation trends, it makes sense, then, to look very closely for signs of similar associations between humans and non-humans. This will, of course, not explain everything – but ignoring this perspective will most certainly result in some key issues being overlooked. This is what motivates some scholars to employ conceptual tools borrowed from STS to better understand some aspects of social tensions in their physical setting.

Despite the fact that Actor-Network Theory (ANT) does not conceptually or semantically distinguish between the social and the material – and likewise between two inverse causal directions between them – the majority of STS scholars still employ these concepts as heuristic tools or 'crutches'. Much has been written, for example, about the 'social shaping' processes of artefacts and, conversely, about their 'social impact'. The latter, which essentially concerns the notion of non-human agency, is one of ANT's most distinctive features and has been encapsulated in the notion that artefacts can contain 'programs' (Latour 1992) 'scripts' (Akrich 1992) or overt and hidden 'agendas' (Brand 2008) that designers can build, deliberately or accidentally, into artefacts. The quintessential example is the speed-bump that 'makes' drivers slow down. A book-length exploration of such mechanisms by Verbeek demonstrates that 'taking social impact seriously' does not necessarily lead onto a slippery slope towards environmental, material or architectural determinism as long as we operate with a highly nuanced understanding of non-human agency. It seems justified to conclude that STS at least does not severely suffer from an underappreciation of matter as we have identified in some of the socio-political literature above. This does not mean, however, that a systematic conversation across the disciplinary fence with colleagues from other departments like environmental psychology, planning or criminology would not reveal additional potentials for a more fine-grained ontology of the impact of material settings on social conditions.

STS is certainly not guilty either of underestimating the various social, political, economic and cultural factors that influence the shape of things. In fact, the majority of articles in STS journals trace the convoluted social history of technologies such as nano-particles, medical apparatuses, bicycles, refrigerators or airplanes. The intellectual handling of such social shaping processes draws inspiration from different schools such as the History of Technology or the Social Construction of Technology (SCOT) (Hughes 1983). They provide not only theoretical frames but also methodological toolkits which direct attention to key issues such as relevant social groups, interpretative flexibility, power differentials, value systems, controversies and their 'closure' in studies of how technologies owe their particular shape to human agency (Pinch and Bijker 1984). In short, STS has the potential to appreciate the messy social dynamics that influence the design of public spaces, buildings, street layouts and cities. In the end, however, it is still insufficient to conduct flawless studies on the social shaping of artefacts without considering their effects – and vice versa (Winner 1993). Rather, it is crucial to watch both sides of Latour's metaphorical tennis court, to embrace the whole 'seamless web'

(Hughes 1988) and to follow Bijker's advice that 'the social shaping of a technical artifact and the social impact of that technical artifact are to be analyzed with the same concepts, within the same frame, and, preferably, even within the same study' (Bijker 1992: 97). Then, and only then, might we be able to achieve a more comprehensive understanding of the 'socio-material'.

This does not yet answer the question whether experience and advice exists on how to employ such a framework for the study of cities. Unfortunately, we cannot report much such precedence but at least a number of influential steps in this direction have been taken. One of the first entries in this small, but growing, library is Aibar and Bijker's study of the extension of Barcelona in which the authors start from an understanding of the city as an

> *enormous artifact [which allows to interpret] the size and distribution of its streets, sidewalks, buildings, squares, parks, sewers, and so on … as remarkable physical records of the sociotechnical world in which the city was developed and conceived. [Simultaneously, the city emerges as] a powerful tool in building new boundaries between the social and the technical and, therefore, in building new forms of life. (Aibar and Bijker 1997: 23)*

Other authors who have made important contributions to a socio-material understanding of the built environment include, in chronological order, Callon (1996), Latour (1998), Söderström (2000), Guy et al. (2001), Moore (2001), Rohracher and Ornetzeder (2002), Moore and Brand (2003), Chatzis and Coutard (2005), Guy and Moore (2005), Hommels (2005), Yaneva (2005), Houdart (2006), Brand (2008). Despite these efforts, scholarly work at the intersection of STS and architecture or urban planning still has not reached a critical mass as Moore and Karvonen recently argued: 'There has been little emphasis in STS scholarship to date on the design of the built environment' (2008: 29).

STS-inspired research about the built environment as product and mediator of socio-political tensions is even scarcer. Again, such efforts are not non-existent as evidenced by sessions at the annual meeting of the European Association for the Study of Science and Technology (EASST) in 2006[4] and at the Joint Conference of the Society for Social Studies of Science and the EASST in 2008.[5] Overall, however, it seems fair to state that STS has a blind spot for the dynamic of polarisation, escalation, radicalisation and de-escalation as interaction between humans and non-humans. This clearly is a missed opportunity, especially if we acknowledge the inherent obduracy of the built environment (Hommels 2005) combined with its ability to 'inadvertently accentuate as much as ameliorate divisions in contested space' (Morrissey and Gaffikin 2006: 877). In other words, the Westlink bridge will probably sit where it sits for the next 40 years although it clearly contributes to (but does not cause) the deterioration of some people's everyday lives. STS has the conceptual equipment to deal with such dynamics more comprehensively than

---

4   Session: 'The Built Environment and Social Practices in Contested Spaces' (Lausanne, 23–26 August 2006).

5   Session: 'Contested and Constructed Spaces: Battles over Territory, Identity, and Resources' (Rotterdam, 20–24 August 2008).

some other disciplines, but as of yet makes little use of it. We suggest that this situation should and could be remedied. To be sure, this is not meant to replace any of the aforementioned approaches; just to complement them.

CONCLUSION:
BRIDGING SOCIAL AND MATERIAL ASPECTS OF POLARISATION

As we write this, renewed attacks on security forces by the Real- and Continuity IRA in Northern Ireland not only have animated debates about the situation of the Peace Agreement, but have also contributed to more mundane and material consequences, such as the resurgence of aggressive graffiti (Bowcott 2009). Evidence such as this or, of course, the Westlink Bridge, demonstrates that social (de-)polarisation is not an a-spatial or a-material phenomenon. Accordingly, we would argue, more integrated approaches are needed to understand and tackle polarisation that consider not only socio-political complexities, but also the material context. Neither of these variables deserves primacy. Rather, their dialectical relationship should be acknowledged and guide the analysis of concrete cases and cities where diversity is not appreciated as asset but cause for tension.

In the four literature families reviewed here, we encountered both theoretical potential and the need for more synergies in grasping the recursive or looping relationship between the material and the social in the context of (de-)polarisation. The war city literature tends to focus on the extreme socio-material recursive processes of the state of war, rather than on more subtle phases of (de-)escalation before and after the explosion of violence. The 'socio-political literature' accounts for mindset, ideology, behaviour and political grievances, but provides little or no evidence of the role of the materiality of such phenomena. The 'built environment literature' (from 1970s determinism to more nuanced recent contributions) focuses on material aspects, but in some instances tends to favour fixed formulas above contextuality. Finally, the STS approach appears as a potentially suitable theoretical platform, even if it rarely deals with conflict-related issues; this and similar topics within STS should develop in parallel to STS's increasing dedication to the built environment and cities as socio-material phenomena.

4

The Belfast Case

CONTEXT

Belfast, the capital of Northern Ireland, has suffered many decades of acrimonious troubles between its Loyalist and Republican citizens, with the British state, its police force and its army caught in between and often disliked by both parties. The quarrels in Northern Ireland have deep historical roots which deserve and require book-length explanations. What is indispensable as background understanding is the constitutional question, that is, the unresolved dispute over the national belonging of the north-eastern part of the island of Ireland. Many Catholics, Nationalists and Republicans argue that it should be part of the Republic of Ireland. Conversely, many Protestants, Unionists and Loyalists claim that it is a legitimate part of the United Kingdom.

These two ethnic, religious and partly also linguistic groups have never been evenly spread across the territory of Belfast. This spatial clustering became more pronounced during the city's industrial heyday when the accelerated need for manual labour drew many Catholic families from rural parts of the island to the boom town in the north-east where they tended to settle either in proximity to the existing Irish community or wherever space was available, which was largely in the west of the city. While some physical barriers separating the two communities were built in the early twentieth century, they were never a prominent feature of Belfast's urban fabric. This changed in 1969 when a phase of extremely violent atrocities, known as 'The Troubles', erupted. Bombing campaigns, street battles and arson attacks against '25,000 households' (Calame and Charlesworth 2009: 80) triggered the exodus of thousands of families from relatively mixed areas into the heartland of 'their' community, which resulted not only in collective trauma, deep-seated hatred and a seemingly hereditary mistrust, but also in a staggering degree of segregation. In 2005, the percentage of Belfast's population living in severely segregated wards (whose population is 90 per cent or more homogeneous by religion) was 55.4 per cent (Morrissey and Gaffikin 2006: 881). This situation is graphically depicted in maps 4.1 and 4.2.

Map 4.1
The geographical
focus of Protestant
residential areas
is in the eastern
parts of Belfast;
but also in one
segment (Shankill)
of the west. The
north-west is
a patchwork
of Catholic/
Protestant areas.

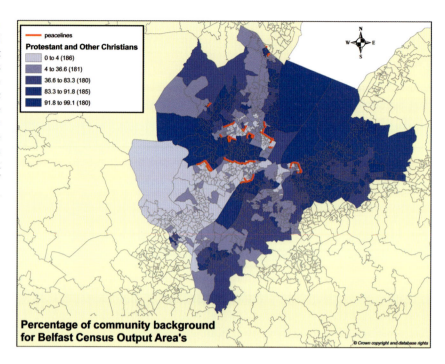

Map 4.2
Catholic
settlements in
Belfast are
mostly found in
the south-western
and north-western
parts of Belfast.
Quite often,
trouble erupts
in locations
where Catholic
and Protestant
residential
areas meet.

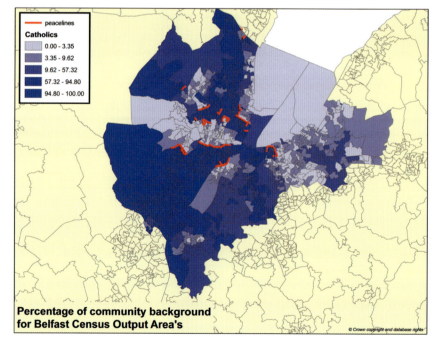

Luckily, things have moved on. In April 1998 the so-called 'Good Friday Agreement' was struck and subsequently approved by over 70 per cent of the Northern Irish electorate. It set the trajectory for the transfer of political powers from London to a new directly elected Northern Ireland Assembly, which finally became operational in 2007. Political violence is not a staple of daily news any more and the major paramilitary groups have officially put down their weapons. Although there is by far no agreement on many issues, at least disagreements are now mostly channelled into the political arena.

> Most of the mixed areas in Belfast are all middle-class areas because people's concern is their property's value. It's not who they live next door to, as long as your next door neighbour looks after their property as well. You don't particularly care what colour, creed, religion they are. (Interviewee Bel-25)

Still, many people we spoke to argued that politicians are lagging a long way behind the willingness for reconciliation of many people doing cross-community work on the ground. Bollens' (2012) analysis seems to confirm this because he concludes that a significant number of politicians still use sectarian rhetoric to strengthen their profile as unyielding hardliners among their conservative constituencies. Conversely, the fact that the newly formed Police Service Northern Ireland (the renamed and reforged successor to the Royal Ulster Constabulary) is regularly more than busy quelling or controlling local skirmishes, brawls and riots signals that some sections of the population are lagging behind the, more or less enthusiastic, compromises of politicians. In fact, Bollens reports 'this is a "peace" that feels qualitatively different from what people thought and hoped peace would feel like' (2012: 57). Such was the situation when we conducted our fieldwork in Belfast in the summer of 2008.

DEFENSIVE ARCHITECTURE/PEACELINES

Many urban artefacts in Belfast owe their existence, shape and sometimes even colour to this socio-political condition. Most notorious are probably the 88 'security and segregation barriers', some of them known as so-called peace walls, separating Catholic from Protestant communities (see the red lines in maps 4.1 and 4.2). These barriers are made of concrete, brick or corrugated metal (Figure 4.1), often with barbed wire on top, and extend up to 1.6 kilometres in length and 12 metres in height.

One particular exemplars of a peace wall is the one along Cupar Street (Figure 4.2), which has acquired a questionable degree of renown because it is included as touristic sight in many city tours.

Figure 4.1
Peace walls are
often constructed
from concrete,
corrugated metal
and fencing;
and require
maintenance

Figure 4.2
The Protestant side
of the Cupar Street
peace wall, may
be one of the most
drastic examples
of how the built
environment
mirrors the socio-
political condition
in Belfast; but also
how it mediates
the social by
keeping people
on both sides
rigorously apart

Depending on the availability of alternative space, houses have sometimes to be built – or come to be located – very near such peace walls. Figure 4.3 shows such a situation on the Catholic side of the Cupar Street peace wall – visible on the far right of the image.

Figure 4.3
Double- and
triple-protected
backyards facing
the Cupar Street
peace wall

Due to different housing pressures in Protestant and Catholic areas, residences in the latter are typically built much closer to peace walls and need, in many cases, extra protection if the height of the peace wall does not suffice to stop all ballistic attacks reliably. The spatial situation on the protestant side of the Cupar Street peace wall is significantly more relaxed (Figure 4.4).

However, in some cases Protestant houses are also overshadowed by a peace wall as in the case of Cluan Place (Figure 4.5) in the Catholic enclave of Short Strand within the wider, predominately Protestant, area of East Belfast (urban context at http://tinyurl.com/bu4ukp2).

Figure 4.4
Cupar Street
Loyalist houses
across the road
from the peace
wall. The peace
wall is not the blue
fence but behind
the photographer.

Figure 4.5
The peace wall
around Cluan
Place had to be
built very close to
the houses but the
residents learned
to lead more or
less normal lives

Even Alexandra Park, theoretically a recreational asset in North Belfast, had to be divided by a wall (Figure 4.6), mainly in order to separate young people from the two adjacent neighbourhoods in search of the thrill they derive from 'recreational rioting'.

Figure 4.6
The wall
separating
Alexandra Park.
This is even visible
on Google Maps
at http://tinyurl.
com/7sa3ooq.

But everyday life goes on. People need to go shopping, see a doctor, post a letter, exercise in a gym. A large array of such services therefore exists in duplicate throughout Belfast's urban fabric. Certain shopping malls, for example, are located at the heart of single-identity areas, thus reducing the necessity to cross sectarian boundaries, and the likelihood of having one's stereotypes of the 'others' challenged. Duplicating services and infrastructures is, of course, not a sign of rational planning but regrettable reality in parts of Northern Ireland. This spatial inefficiency also applies to many post offices and amenities provided by the city council like community centres with detrimental impacts on municipal finances.

Segregated neighbourhoods must not become severed though because the parallel universes can never, and should not, be entirely autarkic. The location of many jobs, for example, follows real estate logic much more than sectarian preferences. For these and many other reasons, peace walls need to be permeable to some degree. This is achieved by a series of gates (Figure 4.7) which are open during quiet times of the year and day. During the night or other trouble-prone periods they can be shut either by the police or representatives of the adjacent communities. Some gates also open and close on a regular schedule and thus can even influence something as mundane as people's commuting patterns.

Some peace walls are also punctuated by pedestrian gates. A particular social arrangement has been established around the one along Duncairn Gardens (Figure 4.8), where the nearby pharmacist is also the gatekeeper who can unlock the gate in order to provide patients from the other side access to urgently needed drugs. The urban context of this site is available on Google Maps at http://tinyurl.com/7y5x472.

Figure 4.7
Gate in a peace
wall to facilitate
vehicular flow

Figure 4.8
Pedestrian gate
along Duncairn
Gardens

Not all physical barriers take the shape and form of a monumental wall. In many cases they appear as fences of varying height, length, sturdiness and design. The latter point is quite important because in certain situations it can make quite a difference whether a fence is visually permeable (see-through). This determines the degree to which human surveillance is possible; or whether someone can hide at an angle to a presumed observer. The existence and strength of horizontal bars within a fence meshing can also be important because they can make it easier or more difficult for someone to climb over the fence. Figure 4.35 further below show examples of such considerations. Most fences in Belfast, however, are not characterised by particularly elaborate design logics. Typically, their main quality is sturdiness, robustness and height, all of which depend on the purpose in every specific location (see Figure 4.9).

Figure 4.9 North Queen Street. The fact that the high section of the fence stops suddenly indicates that the far end of the image is near a typical trouble hotspot and that its main purpose is primarily against opportunistic and not premeditated attacks.

The manifestation of conflict in Belfast is not only visible and tangible in the form of dividing objects that keep the two communities apart. Also the design of houses, neighbourhoods and streets can be a symptom of underlying social tensions. The same is true for the orientation of windows or the decision of which plants to grow in one's garden. As can be seen in Figure 4.10, the windows of houses near peace walls or near typical riot places are often protected with extra metal grills.

Heavy fortification or defensive architecture can also be found at very many police stations as representatives of the British state, loathed by most Republicans (Figure 4.11).

In many cases, such 'target hardening' approaches are complemented with measures to deter attacks in the first place. Most prominently, this happens through CCTV surveillance, which raises the density of cameras even above the already high level of the UK at large. Ironically, such equipment needs to be protected itself in many locations (Figure 4.12).

In certain hotspots where members of the warring communities (mainly young males) typically clash, forests of fortified poles with CCTV cameras on top (Figure 4.13) mirror Belfast's peculiar socio-political situation.

Figure 4.10
The proximity to a
peace wall – seen
between the two
houses – requires
extra protective
equipment, here
for the windows

Figure 4.11
Police station
in Belfast

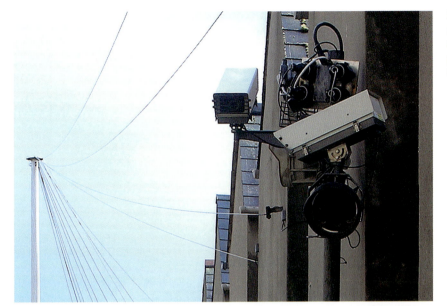

Figure 4.12
A CCTV camera, meant to protect, in need of protection

Figure 4.13
A series of fortified CCTV poles dominates the intersection between Limestone Road and Newington Street. Urban context at http://tinyurl.com/ch4rk28.

Growing up (Leonard 2010) and living in such an urban environment doubtlessly has an impact on the (ir)regularity with which mutual stereotypes can be challenged through direct encounters with 'the others'. Bollens writes in this context that 'learning of stereotypes feels easier and even natural if you do not know the other person' (2012: 61). For this and many other reasons, we would therefore argue that the material shape of a divided city not only reflects (mirrors) but also influences (mediates) the lived reality of the division.

MURALS AND POLITICAL SYMBOLS

Most of the above examples are, in one way or another, 'corporeal'; they 'talk to the body'; their effect rests on some kind of impact on a human being's physical existence, the fact that humans reflect light, have limited muscle power and cannot fly. Many artefacts and elements of the urban environment can be found in Belfast that belong to a different, more semiotic category. Their effect rests on their meaning and only affects those who are able to decipher this meaning. At the most basic level this requires the ability to read. In most cases, however, the actual words or images require further interpretation and de-coding skills which rely on knowledge about Northern Ireland's history, symbolic conventions, idioms and so forth. Murals are clearly the most frequent and most visible form of this kind of urban artefact. In fact, Belfast is famous for its hundreds of murals, ranging in artistic quality from quick tags to elaborate paintings and in their message from intimidating, aggressive, protective, revengeful, triumphalist, educational, celebratory, solidarity, etc.

Figure 4.14
A dramatic visual display of the determination to defend a particular community

Figure 4.15
A number of
Republican murals
depict solidarity
with people from
other parts of
the world that
they perceive as
similarly oppressed
by illegitimate
occupiers

Figure 4.16
A number
of murals
commemorate
the heroes of
a particular
community; here
Bobby Sands, an
IRA activist who
died on hunger
strike in 1981

Figure 4.17
A mural of another
mural, doubling
as advertisement
for a local taxi
company

Figure 4.18
This Catholic mural
deliberately keeps
the psychological
wounds open
which were
afflicted during the
Holy Cross dispute
in 2001 and 2002
which involved
school children

Figure 4.19
The 'Good Friday
Agreement'
was signed on
20 May 1998.
Some obviously
did not like its
conciliatory nature.

Figure 4.20
Paramilitary
organisations, here
the Ulster Freedom
Fighters, display
their (real or
desired) presence

Figure 4.21 Although outlawed, a number of paramilitary organisations display their presence in certain areas with flags, sometimes mounted hastily with duct tape to lamp posts

Figure 4.22 A mural in honour of the Queen Mother; not aggressive but clearly a strong statement on the 'constitutional question'

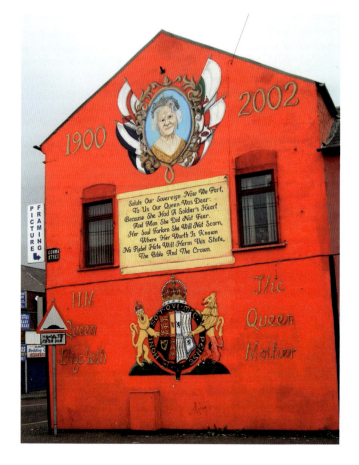

Not only walls but also kerb-stones can serve as a suitable canvass where one's allegiance can be displayed (Figure 4.23). In a number of areas of Belfast they are painted in the national colours of the residents' identity: Blue, white and red in Protestant areas; green, white and orange in Catholic ones. However, they do not simply mirror identity but effectively intimidate 'others'. In areas close to the city centre they also attract tourists.

Figure 4.23
Painted kerb-stones, here in the colours of the British flag

Figure 4.24
Bilingual street signs are often perceived as natural by a linguistic minority whereas they can be anathema to the majority

In recent years, a large number of community workers and volunteers try to quell the psychological reproduction of hatred through a plethora of initiatives for the children of Belfast. This includes attempts to tackle the most aggressive and inflammatory murals and to replace them through cross-community initiatives with more amicable or at least neutral alternatives (Figure 4.25).

Figure 4.25 A somewhat blitheful, but still implicitly sectarian, painting by children near the Short Strand peace wall

Figure 4.26 A mural in East Belfast commemorating the football star George Best

Where such efforts make use of Belfast's tradition and expertise in mural painting, the result can be very artistic. The Belfast-born football star George Best, who died in 2005, is an ideal motive for such initiatives (Figure 4.26) because he is accepted as hero of a different kind by both communities.

What also unites every adult in Belfast is the need of employment and fair pay. These issues motivated massive cross-community action in 1907 during the famous Belfast Dock strike which saw a rare degree of Catholic–Protestant solidarity. This event was recently chosen as the motive for a new mural on a road connecting the staunchly Catholic Falls Road with the Protestant stronghold along Shankill Road (Figure 4.27). This visual reminder is meant to stimulate the acknowledgement of similarly shared concerns in the twenty-first century, of which there are many.

Figure 4.27 Mural about the strike of Belfast's dock workers of 1907. Urban context at http://tinyurl. com/cns64uj.

STEWARTSTOWN ROAD REGENERATION PROJECT

Luckily, a so-called peace process is under way in Northern Ireland and the consensus that the future should be non-violent is fairly robust. This goal is not easily implemented in hearts, minds and on the ground, however, and part of the problem certainly lies in the obduracy of the built environment. Nevertheless, successful attempts can be reported to remove a few security fences, gates and road barriers. Yet more ambitious than the removal of architecture that keeps people apart is the establishment of material structures that bring people together.

The Stewartstown Road Regeneration Project (SRRP; www.stewartstownroad. org) in outer West Belfast is such an attempt. It deserves extra attention, not least because it is often portrayed as a model that inspires various other grassroots, non-governmental and state organisations in their efforts towards de-polarisation and de-radicalisation.

SRRP is located at the interface between the Protestant enclave of Suffolk and the predominantly Catholic area Lenadoon. The Stewartstown Road was the site of countless violent clashes between these two groups, the police and the British Army over several decades and was therefore fortified with a peace wall, intended to keep the warring factions apart. Life in Suffolk was seen by many residents as an existence under siege. Those with the strongest determination or who lacked alternatives felt like the last Mohicans. Many of those who could, however, had moved to a more tranquil life in the suburbs. As a result, many houses in Suffolk were vacant and derelict (Figure 4.28).

Figure 4.28
Some of the many
derelict houses
in the Protestant
Suffolk enclave.
They are mostly
demolished now.

Also the small row of shops (with unused maisonettes) had only two retail units rented out and was anything but a community asset (figures 4.29 and 4.30).

> *Suffolk identified the peaceline as a safeguard, as a guarantee of its future through the control of its own territory. Lenadoon did not need this type of guarantee. So both communities saw in the peaceline a device to block trouble, but Suffolk also saw in it a guarantee of existence. (Interviewee Bel-81)*

Over the last 10 years, however, courageous individuals – many of whom are women – from both sides took the initiative to develop a more peaceful relationship between their communities. After many years of negotiations, disputes, highs and lows, their efforts resulted in the construction of a jointly owned and managed two-storey building (figures 4.31 and 4.32), replacing the old row of shops. Its roughly 1,000 square metres accommodate offices for community groups, four retail units and commercially let office space. The scheme is widely considered a financial and social success with a long waiting list for the retail units, general acceptance among most residents of the adjoining communities, absence of sectarian graffiti and income generation for community initiatives. This experience energised the construction of a second phase, which extended the building by two more retail units, more office space and a separate nursery. The urban context during the construction of phase II can be seen at http://tinyurl.com/cjv2ydc.

Figure 4.29
Semi-derelict
shops and
maisonettes –
1999 (front)

Figure 4.30
Semi-derelict
shops and
maisonettes –
1999 (rear)

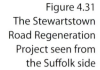

Figure 4.31
The Stewartstown
Road Regeneration
Project seen from
the Suffolk side

Figure 4.32
The Stewartstown
Road Regeneration
Project seen from
the Lenadoon side

Technically, the SRRP building is still part of a peace wall. Its continuation, directly adjacent to the SRRP building, can be seen in Figure 4.33.

The SRRP building can therefore not do without metal bollards, CCTV cameras, anti-graffiti coating, toughened window glass, etc. (example in Figure 4.34). The experience so far, however, shows that they are hardly tested.

Figure 4.35 shows two different types of fences (sturdy versus see-through), chosen for the two different construction phases of SRRP because the perception of the likely threat has changed. This is a clear example of how materiality mirrors the social situation.

Another example of the target-hardening approach can be seen in Figure 4.36. It shows the front façade of the nursery, which was built as part of SRRP's phase II. The round windows are meant to make a friendly impression but the need to protect them with metal roller shutters turned out as quite an engineering challenge.

Figure 4.33
The Suffolk side of the peace wall, directly adjacent to the SRRP building (on the left). Stewartstown Road is behind the gate and the Catholic community of Lenadoon on the other side of the road (buildings in background).

Figure 4.34
A reinforced fence was chosen to connect the long commercial building of SRRP to the nursery in order to reflect the complex's continued function as a peace wall

Figure 4.35
Two different
types of fences
reflect different
social situations

Figure 4.36
The SRRP nursery
with its friendly
but protected
windows

What is less conventional and more interesting are other architectural features of the SRRP building, which do not simply harden it as a potential target. Among the design characteristics that make it particularly suitable as a shared space is the decision to create two main entrances; one each from the Lenadoon and the Suffolk side, connected by a corridor on the ground floor (figures 4.37 and 4.38).

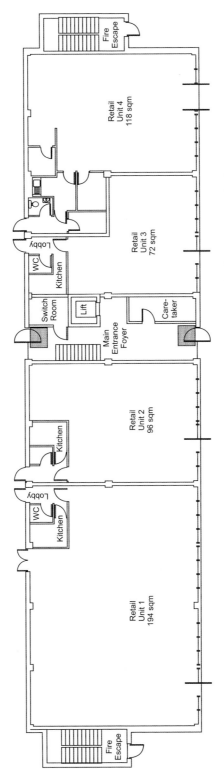

Figure 4.37 Ground floor of SRRP, phase I, showing the corridor that connects both communities in the centre

How do we notice a proper shared space? … How do we know that this is a shared space? What does the management look like? What does the governance look like? What do the services look like? How do we put in measures to make sure that the organisation partner delivers on real objectives of shared space? (Interviewee Bel-73)

Figure 4.38 The corridor connecting the Suffolk and the Lenadoon entry/exit of the building. That way, anyone can enter/exit the building from their 'own'/'safe' side.

This, and the identical type of doors, address and house number on both sides (Figure 4.39), underlines the architectural and symbolic non-discrimination and non-preference of either community.

Figure 4.39 SRRP's Lenadoon side (left) and Suffolk side (right) door

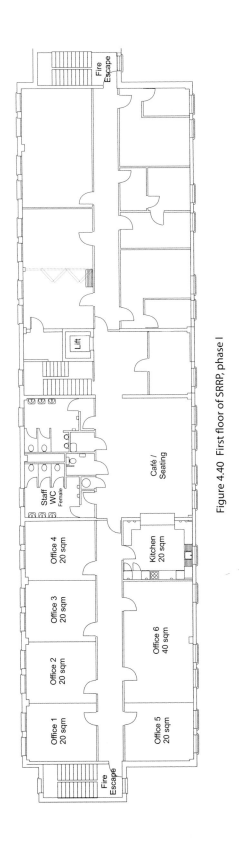

Figure 4.40 First floor of SRRP, phase I

The principle of equal treatment is also visible and tangible on the first floor. Its north-eastern (left on the floorplan, Figure 4.40) half is commercially rented out, the other used by community groups. The shape of the rooms in the right bottom part shows the importance of material fairness, for example with identical L-shaped offices. The architect proposed this design only after complaints about an earlier draft, which had not followed the equal treatment logic to the same degree.

> Stewartstown Road didn't have that huge physical barrier. The old building was still a permeable barrier. At other peacelines they are absolute. You could walk across the road and be on the other territoriality. There were already stores that were used from both sides. You can replicate the process but the geographical setting is not similar elsewhere. Even the most cynical one would say that's truly shared space. I can't think of anything else that is quite similar. (Interviewee Bel-23a)

All of SRRP's efforts and effects have not eroded the identity of either community. This was never the intention any way. It is not about syncretism but about co-existence. Youths in Suffolk still gather anything combustible in early July in preparation of the 12 July bonfire to commemorate a historical victory over Catholic King James in 1690 (Figure 4.41). And while their neighbours in Lenadoon might not applaud this, one can now see them wearing green GAA jerseys (a clear sign of Catholicism) on SRRP premises and sharing a coffee with a Suffolk resident – and vice versa. Before SRRP, the infrastructure – and underlying trust-building process – simply did not exist for this to happen.

Figure 4.41 Preparing for the 12 July bonfire in Suffolk. A sign of Protestant community pride and identity, just 100 metres away from SRRP.

The massive and brave efforts for the establishment of SRRP were honoured in 2003 with the British Urban Regeneration Association's award for best practice in community regeneration.

> One of the bigger issues was actually this area at the rear of the site, going back to the idea that it was a peace line. We always had to bear in mind that the peace line isn't a permanent thing and it may well come down, so there was always a way of looking at this scheme that even though it is built on this secure line, that it wouldn't necessarily always be that way. (Interviewee Bel-25)

5

The Beirut Case

CONTEXT

Beirut, the capital of multi-sectarian Lebanon is often described as a city cyclically destroyed and rebuilt, by natural disaster (such as the earthquake and tsunami that razed this city in AD 551) or by conflict (Fregonese 2009, 2012a). Popular literature frequently evokes images of Beirut as a place of periodical rebirth and reconstruction from chronic conflict: 'Beirut is back', 'Beirut the Phoenix rises from its ashes', we read in travel magazines, in-flight brochures and fashion weeklies. This cycle of destruction/reconstruction is also reflected by the numerous urban scars provoked by different political crises and very often is commodified within regeneration projects in war-torn or brand new neighbourhoods (Figure 5.1).

Figure 5.1
Panels surrounding a construction site in 2010, celebrating the most recent of Beirut's rebirths: The new waterfront of Zaitunay Bay

Since its independence in 1943 and among geopolitical changes in the region, Lebanon endured both intra-state politico-confessional conflicts (1952, 1958, 1975–90) and the presence of foreign armies on its territory (in 1976, 1978, 1982, 2006). After a phase of relatively peaceful post-war redevelopment (1990–2005), the assassination of former Prime Minister Rafiq al-Hariri in February 2005 profoundly changed the country's political equilibrium. Most importantly, it triggered unprecedented mass demonstrations – the 'Cedar Revolution' or 'Beirut's Spring' – which successfully demanded the withdrawal of Syrian troops present in Lebanon since 1976. Lebanese internal politics, however, soon polarised along new political axes.[1] Following a string of episodes of urban violence, more serious clashes between opposed armed groups exploded during the early weeks of May 2008. In what were the worst weeks of internal violence since the civil war, dozens of people died and hundreds were injured including civilians, armed militants and regular soldiers. While an agreement brokered by Qatar brought back a degree of stability, at least up to the Arab uprisings of 2011–12, several signs of deep-seated communal distrust have remained visible and tangible in Beirut. This context underpinned our visit in January 2009.

LAYERS

In Beirut, numerous urban artefacts express consecutive periods of tension and polarisation and co-exist with attempts to create shared spaces in what is still, in many aspects, a divided city (Calame and Charlesworth 2009). Perhaps the most strikingly visual indicator of Beirut's intervals of conflict and pacification are the pockets of material dereliction and destruction scarring Beirut's urban fabric. In contrast to the detailed reports of the damage caused by the 2006 Israeli invasion (Amnesty International 2006; Human Rights Watch 2006), assessments of damage to infrastructure during the Lebanese civil war are rare and far from comprehensive (Labaki and Abou Rjeily 1993). Controversies surrounding the memory of the civil war have also prevented the creation of a shared historiography of that period, which as a consequence led to 'the absence of a unified understanding of the city' (Fawaz and Peillen 2003: 1). Infrastructural *duplication* is a dramatic and costly aspect of division in many conflictual cities (Calame and Charlesworth 2009; Gaffikin and Morrissey 2011). In Beirut, however, due to the variety of militias and the micro-territorialities of the long civil war, the city has been reshaped through a *multiplication* of basic infrastructures: not only schools, hospitals and other basic services, but also artefacts like water and gas tanks, electricity generators and wires.

---

1   The political rift divides two main camps: March 14 and March 8. The former opposes any Syrian influence in Lebanon and is generally pro-Western and pro-Saudi; the latter seconds Syria and Iran, with Hezbollah as leading party. While March 14 had the parliamentary majority at different points from 2005, in January 2011 a March 8-backed government took power.

During the (Civil) War, people developed all kinds of survival strategies and this included material aspects. For example, people installed backup-systems for water, electricity, etc. They arranged places where they could take refuge so they would know where to run in the worst case; they moved their beds from one side of the building to the other; they knew when to open the window so that the air pressure of explosions would not burst them; they started to systematically replace all wooden house-doors with steel doors to turn their home into a fortress. (Interviewee Bei-1)

The construction of private gated developments both during and after the civil war (Glasze 2003) contributed to normalise segregated and defensive architectures (Figure 5.2). That infrastructural imprint still shapes contemporary access to resources and right to the city (Fawaz and Deboulet 2011), resulting in a disjointed urban landscape.

Figure 5.2 Urban disjunctions. Next to some derelict building, a new gated residential development – surrounded by a high concrete wall – has recently been completed in the Hamra neighbourhood west of the Beirut Central District (BCD). Both during and after the civil war, the construction of privately owned gated developments has thrived in Beirut and surroundings.

Wartime destruction is visible particularly along the former wartime line of confrontation (the Green Line) stretching from south to north cutting through the city centre. Buildings near the former Green Line are riddled with bullet holes, some of them inhabited (Figure 5.3). Here, the disjuncture in the urban fabric appears even starker because these buildings are situated near the newly reconstructed, shiny BCD, just a few minutes' walk away: a space for expensive international retail, leisure, luxury residences, offices and the official state institutions.

Figure 5.3 Buildings near the former Green Line are still riddled with bullet holes, but inhabited, typically by lower income families. The BCD, with its expensive international retail chains, is just 10 minutes' walk away.

Figure 5.4 A street in the BCD, where perfectly restored buildings, mainly from the French mandate period, stand just a few minutes' walk away from the dereliction of the former Green Line. The BCD was officially developed into a 'neutral' space for all, regardless of their political, religious or ethnic background. Some argue that it created new socio-economic divisions because not many can afford the luxury goods offered there.

DEMARCATIONS

Prominent and almost ubiquitous signs of polarisation in Beirut are political posters, flags and graffiti – often made using easily replicable stencils – that demonstrate the real or intended territorial presence, even dominance, of a particular political party.

> All the quarters had their own political iconic patterns. Even in the same buildings: on the one floor you will have a picture of Joumblat [a political leader of the Druze community] and on the other floor you will have the picture of Hezbollah, and the neighbours fight for putting up the pictures and the pictures get bigger. (Interviewee Bei-22)

This was a common practice during wartime (Chakhtoura 2005; Maasri 2008), but it persists today even before the conflict becomes open. In times of heightened tensions the presence of these artefacts becomes problematic, and is sometimes the target of de-escalating interventions. For example, after the 2008 clashes, authorities and political leaders in the Beirut municipal area agreed to remove or paint over political posters and graffiti around the city, aiming to end what had become a race of plastering the city with political statements (Figure 5.5).

Figure 5.5
As a measure of reducing potential for provocation and conflict, key political leaders agreed to remove sectarian symbols and posters from the Beirut municipal area in 2008. In this illustration, the Amal party circular symbol has been painted over in white.

Religious artefacts like shrines or statues are prominent indicators of belonging and religious territoriality. While some demarcations are visible and concrete and thus 'talk to the body' in a very direct way even to outsiders, the effects of many others rest on symbolic meanings requiring a degree of local knowledge and de-coding. A group of students from the Lebanese University involved in our participatory photography activity, took several pictures of religious markers in the neighbourhood of Shiyyah/Ayn Remmane in the southern periphery of the city. Here, neighbourhoods respectively affiliated with the opposing parties Amal (Shia Muslim) and Lebanese Forces (Christian) are densely punctuated by religious-political markers. Granite reproductions of the pietas (Figure 5.6), wooden crosses, fabric banners of Maronite Christians' founding saint Maroun, graffiti and posters of party leaders populate the Christian side, while marble shrines, oversized reproductions of imams (Figure 5.7) and Muslim martyrs' posters are replicated dozens of times along a highway on the Muslim side. Religious and political markers are often found next to each other (Figure 5.8).

Figure 5.6 Religious and political markers in Ayn er Remmane. A granite statue of the passion of the Christ stands in front of a wooden cross. On the balcony to the left, the Lebanese national flag waves next to the Lebanese Forces party flag.

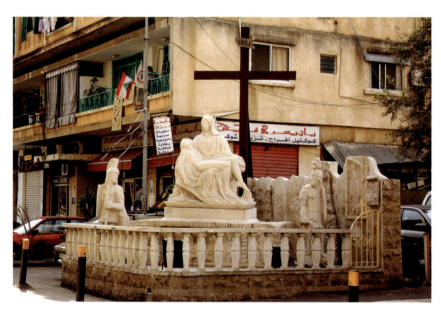

We are in a Christian neighbourhood close to the [former] green line. The invasive sculpture is part of the public space facing the other side of the green line … The scale of the sculpture and its location goes beyond religious representations to constitute a physical barrier at the entrance of the area. (Participatory photography project member, Lebanese University)

Figure 5.7
The entrance to the neighbourhood of Al-Shiyyah: Oil barrels demarcate its entrance, while in the background hangs an oversized portrait of spiritual leader Imam Mussa al-Sadr and a martyrs' shrine

Figure 5.8
Memorial to former Lebanese president Bashir Gemayel in the traditionally Christian neighbourhood of Ashrafieh. Bashir Gemayel was the leader of the right-wing Kata'eb party in the 1980s. He was assassinated in Beirut in September 1983. A huge banner is showing the Virgin Mary in the background.

Religious buildings are also perceived as controversial territorial markers – a feature that we observed also in the Amsterdam case (Chapter 7), regarding the construction of mosques. Some interviewees, for example, perceived the recently built Mohammad al Amin mosque in the BCD (Figure 5.9), commissioned by slain former Prime Minister Rafiq al Hariri, as reclaiming the supposedly neutral BCD area for the Sunni community, in ways that 'do … not help to display [the] neutrality of Solidere'[2] (interviewee Bei-8). The new mosque, according to some interviewees, is too 'overwhelming and underused. It is a blunt political statement' (interviewee Bei-3).

Figure 5.9 Religious buildings provoke different feelings in central Beirut. A new mosque was built in the mid-2000s by the Hariri family and stands next to the Saint George Maronite cathedral. For some, this image represents harmonious co-existence in the neutral space of the BCD. For critics, however, such a demonstrative religious building at such a prominent location is not the most sensitive move, especially with regards to its scale compared to its neighbour.

_____

2   Private company in charge of the reconstruction of the BCD.

Not only is [the mosque] big: the fact that it was built east of the main Cathedral [in Beirut] means that the Christians in the east [of the city] cannot see 'their' main religious building any more. (Interviewee Bei-13)

DEFENSIVE ARCHITECTURE

New demarcations resulting from the post-2005 political condition are shaping Beirut's urban everyday life, specifically those related to security. Surveillance and security technologies nowadays are hardly a feature exclusive to conflictual societies alone, and have become part of a more pervasive military urbanism (Graham 2010). In Beirut, more interestingly, the installation and management of security infrastructure is by no means the prerogative of a sovereign state, but of a constellation of state, non-state and private actors (Fregonese 2012b) resulting in the fragmentation of the territory and of the sovereignty of the city into 'security zones' in the interest of this or that political faction. Everyday urban life in contemporary Beirut is therefore characterised by an extensive apparatus of artefacts of security and surveillance. Sand-bagged army posts (Figure 5.10), surveillance cameras, forests of barbed wire and road barriers (figures 5.11, 5.12 and 5.13) mark many boundaries between different population groups.

Figure 5.10
Makeshift sandbag post of the Lebanese Army at the Sodeco Square junction

More recently, enclaves developed around the highly fortified residences of political leaders enforced by barriers, inspection tents and armed guards. Some of the many objects which owe their existence to the socio-political situation in Lebanon are very hard, physical, almost brutal and unyielding, like metal barriers, checkpoints and barricades. Their use, location, appearance or relaxation are indicators of the levels of tension. In the Beirut Central District, dismantled metal barriers near the United Nations' ESCWA (Economic and Social Commission for Western Asia) building lie on the ground. Some argue that the removal of such devices indicates a trust in the stability of the political situation, however, even when unused, such security artefacts scatter the city centre and their obduracy (Hommels 2005) is sometimes all too present to the body as well as the mind: How long will it take to 'unbuild' the security apparatus of downtown Beirut?

Figure 5.11
Rising barriers
in use near the
United Nations'
ESCWA building
in the BCD during
a protest tent
city in 2006

Lines of demarcation and security zones that emerged during the civil war are overlapping with those erected during more recent political developments. These overlaps are visible materially in the routine inspection for bombs placed under cars. Mirrors – some very makeshift as the one in Figure 5.14 – can be seen at the car entrance to many private and public premises.

Even in the BCD – the place supposed to have developed into the post-war neutral 'space for all', regardless of their political, religious or ethnic background – the built environment mirrors the recent crises. Trash bins have been closed due to the continued bomb threats.

One of the reasons for the increase of defensive architectures in the BCD is the phenomenon of the opposition encampment which ground downtown Beirut to a halt between December 2006 and May 2008.

Figure 5.12 In 2009, we found the same barriers dismantled and left on the road side: A sign of de-escalation?

Figure 5.13 Concrete blocks around the government palace, keeping the road traffic at a safe distance

Figure 5.14 Recently, Beirut experienced a wave of car bombs. Car inspection mirrors are now widely used at the gates of private properties.

Figure 5.15
A trash bin near
Martyrs' Square
in downtown. As
Solidere executives
explained to us, it
used to be open
and usable until
Solidere security
decided to close
it, together with
many others,
due to continued
bomb threats.

ENCAMPMENTS

With Tahrir Square as its emblematic expression, the encampment and occupation of urban space has become the most widespread material expression of ongoing political protests in Middle Eastern as well as European and American cities (Fregonese 2013; Ramadan 2013; Wallach 2013). However, the occupation of space for political goals has mirrored socio-political change in Beirut since the Cedar Revolution of 2005. In January 2006, a tent city (figures 5.16 and 5.17) erected by March 8 supporters in front of governmental buildings constituted an enormous material intervention that paralysed the Beirut Central District for 18 months. At the end of the May 2008 clashes, once a national agreement had been brokered with Lebanese officials gathered in the Qatari capital Doha, the tent city was dismantled overnight. Once again, the urban environment mirrored developments at the official political level.

This powerful physical sign of socio-political change reshaped the practices of access, security and perceptions in and around the city centre. One interviewee brought to our attention the pedestrianisation of usually very trafficked and not so pedestrian-friendly urban arteries in and around the BCD, as well as the the cross-sectarian meetings and events taking place in the camp, and the cooperation in managing the security of the site between the occupiers and the security teams of nearby institutional buildings, as well as the Lebanese police.

Figure 5.16
Between 2005 and
2008, a number of
'tent cities' – the
most prominent
of which, built by
the Hezbollah-
led opposition,
protested
against Prime
Minister Siniora's
government –
represented an
enormous material
intervention in
downtown Beirut

Figure 5.17
With the protest
and the installation
of the tent city,
associated
infrastructure
providing
energy, food
and hygiene was
also developed

Figure 5.18
With the protest
and the installation
of the tent city,
associated
infrastructure
providing
energy, food
and hygiene was
also developed

*[After the tents were erected] cars were not allowed in the area, so it became very pedestrian.
People parked on the outside and walked to their offices. (Interviewee Bei-22)*

Figure 5.19
The anti-sectarian
movement
has erected
encampments
around Beirut,
in the wake
of the Arab
uprisings, adding
further material
expressions of
politicisation
(and potential
polarisation?)
to the space
of the Beirut
Central District

In the wake of the Arab uprisings, Lebanon has experienced a renewed wave of protests, materialised in the encampments of the movement against sectarianism (Figure 5.19). Since spring 2011, new and more diffused encampments were erected in multiple locations around the whole city – often near government buildings and ministers' residences – rather than reclaiming symbolic areas like the March 8 encampments did. Is this diffused materiality of protest in Beirut a mirror – perhaps even a prediction – of further political changes lying ahead?

SHARING SPACE

Mending communal tension through urban interventions is one of the practices that the project is set to explore. Beirut provides numerous examples of attempts to make urban space conducive to positive encounters between its many different communities. However, we noticed that this is often achieved by building spaces that avoid disputes – neutral spaces outside politico-sectarian areas (like in the case of the BCD) or cleansed of any identity references so as to prevent causes for disputes (like in the case of Beirut Mall).

Since 2005, however, this neutrality agenda has been challenged by political change, at least in the BCD. The reconstruction of the BCD by the private company Solidere was meant to create 'the most neutral space in postwar Beirut' (Kabbani 1998: 244). Urban design was to provide a space for reviving the social interaction that had broken down with civil war. The preservation of historical sites and original alleyways, the creation of pedestrianised promenades, squares, internal courtyards and public markets, was aimed at providing the opportunity for positive encounters 'without trespassing on one another's turf' (Kabbani 1998: 259). Urban design and furniture also demonstrate this neutrality, by relying on ancient Phoenician signs and artefacts (Figure 5.20). A symbol of the municipality of Beirut, the Phoenician ship and the book are perceived, or at least promoted, as free of sectarian baggage (although Phoenicianism was a mainly Christian nationalist current in the 1930s). However, the Solidere project is criticised for its commercial character which allegedly creates new divisions between those who can and cannot afford the prices of its restaurants and luxury brand shops.

In 2005, the neutrality of the BCD has been re-politicised by demonstrations and subsequent polarisation. At the start of the protests following Hariri's death, the esplanade of Martyrs' Square and its famous statue commemorating those who fought for Lebanon's independence, became the fulcrum of demonstrations supposed to represent all Lebanese. Subsequently however, the March 8 and March 14 movements managed to polarise the BCD, reclaiming respectively Ryad as-Solh Square (nearer the Government Building) and Martyrs' Square (near Al-Amin mosque). The political assassinations of 2005 and 2006 were not only divisive for society, but also changed the look of the built landscape in central Beirut. A large tent on Martyrs' Square hosts the shrine of the late Rafiq al-Hariri. Besides occupying a prominent site in downtown, the shrine has developed new socio-political dynamics of pilgrimage, as groups of visitors come to pay their respects to the slain prime minister and his young bodyguards. Outside the shrine, a digital counter displays the days since Hariri's assassination. This clock is at once a material artefact but also a mean for social negotiation of memory and history (Till 1999): It keeps the wound deliberately open; renews the memory every day and resists healing.

Figure 5.20 Ornamentation on this lamp post uses Phoenician symbols that would not normally alienate any demographic group. The boat and book constitute also the symbol of Beirut municipality.

Figure 5.21
A view of the
Al-Amin mosque
and Rafiq al Hariri's
tomb and shrine
tent from the
Martyrs statue.
To the left of
the shrine tent,
a digital clock
counting the
days from the
assassination is
up and running.

At a few hundred metres' distance, a huge poster of late journalist and newspaper editor Gebran Tueni – killed by a road-side bomb in December 2005 – hangs from the *Al-Nahar* newspaper building. A few metres away, on the other side of the square, is the Kata'eb party headquarters, also displaying a huge poster of one of their leaders, Pierre Gemayel, killed by gunmen in November 2006 (figures 5.22 and 5.23).

Beirut Mall, a shopping mall located in between the neighbourhoods of Al-Shiyyah and Ayn er-Remmane (discussed above) is also an interesting case of space that relies on the the planned neutralisation of community-specific references in this still at least visually divided location. This commercial project, according to its manager, comes with a carefully crafted architectural and interior design in order to demonstrate politico-sectarian neutrality and class equality. For example, its interiors follow a modernist and minimal design without ornamentations or Arabesques, and particular attention is paid during festivities not to display openly religious visual signs and decoration (snowflakes and stars, for example, rather than nativity scenes, are used as Christmas decorations, as shown in Figure 5.24).

Its designers also went to great lengths to avoid the use of colours which could, even remotely, carry politically symbolic meaning. For example, the different floors in the parking garage are indicated by a range of colours that have been chosen avoiding the colours of the various Lebanese parties' symbols.

Figure 5.22
Material mirrors of
the politicisation
of the BCD: Giant
poster depicting
slain MP and
newspaper editor
Gebran Tueni,
hanging from
the headquarters
of newspaper
Al-Nahar

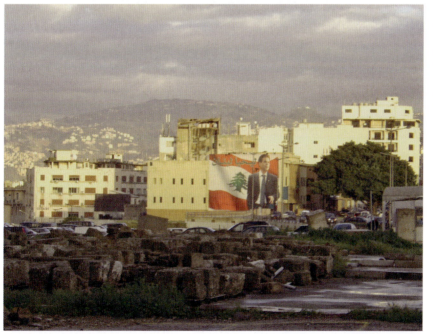

Figure 5.23
Material mirrors of
the politicisation
of the BCD:
Giant poster
depicting slain MP
Pierre Gemayel
hanging from the
headquarters of
the Kata'eb party

Figure 5.24 The architects and decorators of Beirut Mall – which recently opened at an 'interface' between a Christian and a Muslim neighbourhood – took great care to avoid any design tendency, decorative symbols, or colours that could be affiliated with any politico-sectarian group

Figure 5.25
The car park in
Beirut Mall. A
carefully managed
colour scheme that
avoids connections
with political
symbology.

> *Colours are very political in Lebanon. The management (of Beirut Mall) told architects to use neutral colours especially in the parking area. The parking floors need stripes of different colours … to understand on which floor you are. They had to work a lot to come up with mid-tones such as mauve, turquoise, etc. in order to avoid obvious references to political symbols such as orange, yellow, green, and blue. (Interviewee Bei-24)*

Local knowledge and ethnographic research are needed to determine the effectiveness of neutrality in Beirut Mall, which remains an interesting case of attempts to create opportunities for positive encounters. Interestingly, this and similar projects came about not in the altruistic pursuit of community cohesion, but primarily for profit. This does not suggest that commercial motivations are uniquely suited to promote cross-community encounters, but that their potential should be taken into consideration and, where applicable, enrolled.

Whereas the BCD and Beirut Mall are planned interventions aimed at creating neutral space, Beirut's Corniche, a waterfront promenade stretching west of the BCD, constitutes an example of a site of bottom-up conviviality (Delpal 2001), almost traditionally perceived as a space for a varied mix of religious and political backgrounds, where various activities like jogging, swimming, fishing, strolling, sitting and selling take place at different times of the day. A design intervention to promote further conviviality on the waterfront is a series of colourful benches with painted chessboards, and a giant chessboard painted on the waterfront tarmac (Figure 5.26) and, to the best of our knowledge, sponsored by the 'Embellishment Project of the Ain Mreisse Corniche Waterfront Avenue De Paris'. This type of intervention to promote collective interaction and conviviality is strikingly similar to Amsterdam's August Allebeplein and its tables with painted chessboards (Chapter 7).

Figure 5.26
A giant chessboard
has been
painted on the
Corniche tarmac.
An attempt to
attract convivial
interaction that is
strikingly similar
to Amsterdam's
Allebeplein
(see Figure 7.7).

Figure 5.27
Stairs make it
convenient for
shoppers to cross
what used to be
the 'Green Line'.
Small interventions
like these might
could make a
considerable
difference in
people's everyday
lives. The details
of the stairs'
genesis, however,
matter a lot.

Political change in Lebanon is mutually and intimately linked to urban life. The material obduracy of past conflicts layers with new demarcations and defensive architectures and the recently created neutral spaces still pose many questions about their role in the urban management in the face of tension and polarisation in a society where responsible grassroots architecture and micro-scale facilitating interventions (like the one in Figure 5.27) might be more badly needed than grand, 'neutral' projects.

Lastly, Beirut also offers an occasion to reflect on the chances for positive encounters that come from protest encampments and grassroots movements – such as the anti-sectarianism movement – rather than from centralised strategies.

6

The Berlin Case

CONTEXT

What does Berlin have to do with radicalisation and polarisation? After all, it has some of the most ethnically mixed areas in Germany, is not divided by that infamous wall anymore and aspires to become one of the prime pluralist cities in Europe.

The issue here are far-right extremists, allegedly becoming more active, more professional and more radical, especially in certain stronghold areas. In early 2012 – after our fieldwork, which we conducted in September 2008 – the issue of far-right extremism has become a matter of national urgency in Germany; even under the label 'far-right terrorism'. The background to this is the brutal assassination of nine immigrants, one police officer and the execution of bomb attacks against foreigners by the Nationalsozialistischer Untergrund, a small group of neo-Nazis which was touted the 'Brown Army Faction' (after the Red Army Faction, a left-wing extremist terror group of the 1970s).

The situation with far-right extremism in Germany is therefore quite different from the one in Beirut, Belfast and Amsterdam because here we are not dealing with large sections of the population confronting each other. On the contrary, it is a very small minority of 'idiots', as one interviewee said, which stands in opposition to the vast majority of tolerant and law-abiding Berliners – unless, of course, one includes the electoral base of right-wing parties like the National Party of Germany (NPD) which gained up to 14.1 per cent of votes in certain polling stations. Such election results correlate spatially very high with crime scenes of far-right violence and the residential areas of suspected and known action-oriented right-wing extremists (Schmid 2008). All of these are clearly concentrated in the eastern part of Berlin, among them Treptow-Köpenick, Hohenschönhausen and Lichtenberg (Map 6.1). We chose the latter area as case study to investigate whether and how this specific condition plays out materially and spatially in the urban fabric, both as mirror and mediator.

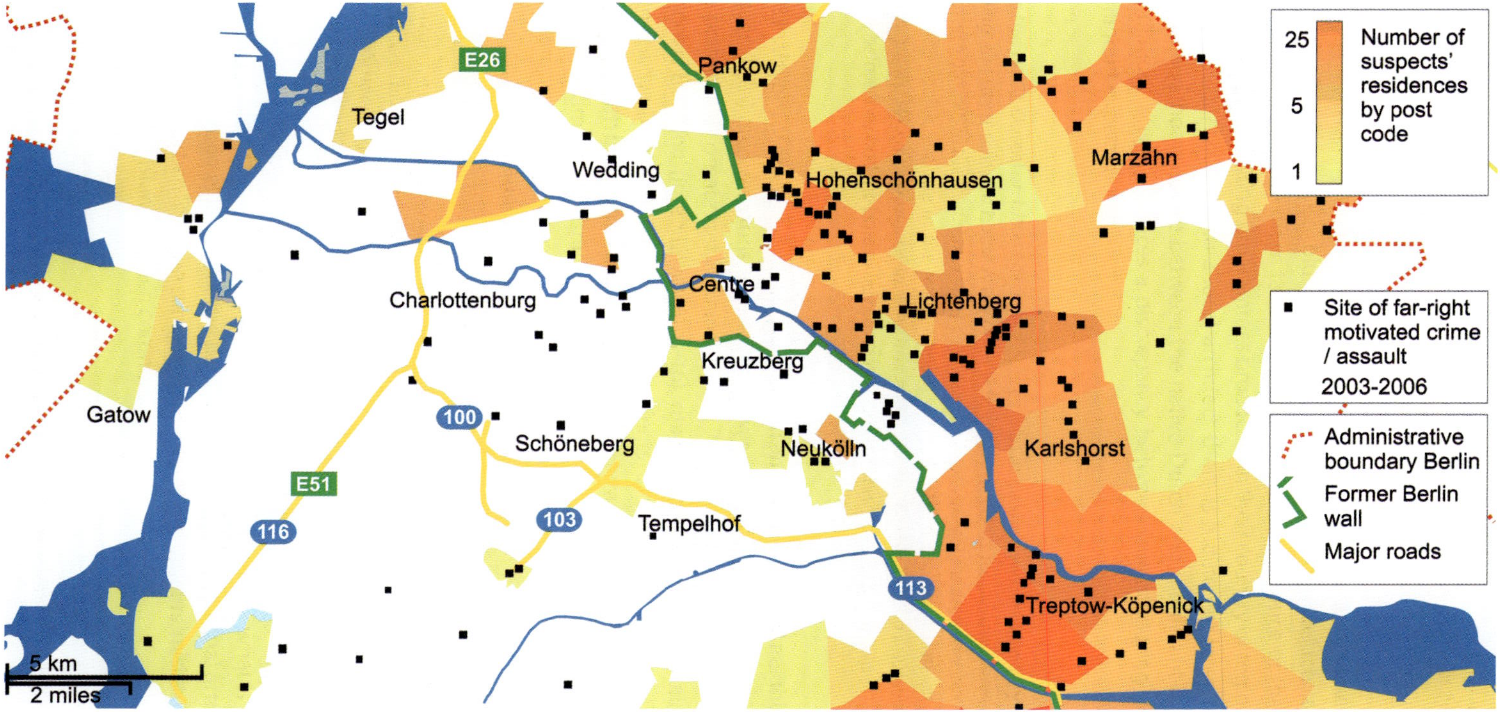

25
5
1
Number of suspects' residences by post code
Site of far-right motivated crime / assault 2003-2006
Administrative boundary Berlin
Former Berlin wall
Major roads
Pankow
Tegel
Wedding
Hohenschönhausen
Marzahn
Charlottenburg
Centre
Lichtenberg
Kreuzberg
Gatow
Schöneberg
Neukölln
Karlshorst
Tempelhof
Treptow-Köpenick
E26
E51
100
103
116
113
5 km
2 miles

Map 6.1 Spatial patterns of illegal far-right activities in Berlin

Another unique characteristic of the Berlin case is that the ideal future most people envisage is not one of mixing and sharing among the contending groups as, for example, in Belfast. In Berlin, the amicable mingling of ordinary Germans, immigrants and neo-Nazis somehow seems not just unachievable but undesirable. Isn't the real goal to eradicate the latter's mindset altogether? From our normative position, we should thus disclose that we have much fewer problems characterising the situation in Berlin as 'radicalisation' and not just as 'polarisation'. As mentioned in Chapter 1, we typically use the former term to describe a situation in which one societal group is clearly more to blame[1] for a breakdown of community cohesion by somehow departing from an ethically desirable 'norm'.

Somewhat unique to the situation in Berlin is also the type of groups involved in the issue, their different motivations, size, legitimacy and capacity to leave material marks on the urban fabric. It is important to bear this in mind when we try to understand who shapes the urban environment, in what ways and with what means:

1. Far-right extremists in different guises: neo-Nazis at different degrees of organisation, professionalisation, determination and brutality, politicians, supporters and voters of certain parties, outspoken agenda-setters and silent followers, xenophobic opportunists, disappointed losers of the German reunification, teenagers under peer pressure, rock bands, etc.
2. Another very outspoken group is the Antifa (anti-fascist) movement, which consists predominantly of activists from the (extreme) left of the political spectrum. Like far-right activists, they, too, lack the financial or legal means to shape the urban environment at the macro- or meso-level.
3. The state, mainly the authorities at the Bezirk level (Berlin consists of 12 administrative units, called Bezirke), private developers and housing corporations exert the strongest influence on the shape of the urban environment. Therefore, even the most notorious far-right stronghold areas look rather normal, at least at the macro-level, which a hasty and superficial inspection would capture.
4. The civil society includes all those not in favour of far-right ideologies but can range from active opponents (just short of Antifa) to those who care very little as long as they are not personally affected by all the trouble. The former help remove right-wing stickers, demonstrate the presence of alternative opinions or publicly display counter-arguments.

> *Many people in Lichtenberg, especially older people, are tolerant towards the extreme right because they live in an old-fashioned ideology from the Third Reich which is hostile to strangers. (Interviewee Ber-28)*

---

1   We do not, however, want to imply that there are no 'idiots' among the opponents of neo-Nazis.

With the exception of the state and private developers none of these groups has the power for large-scale physical interventions in the urban environment. And since Berlin is not, for example, segregated into right-wing and immigrant neighbourhoods – another uniqueness of this case – no one needs to erect high walls between them. The signs of polarisation and radicalisation therefore are not as visible or tangible as in other cities and mainly consist of small, makeshift, cheap and spontaneous artefacts like stickers, posters and graffiti whose effect is mostly based on their symbolic meaning rather than any corporeal property.

We focused on the Bezirk of Lichtenberg (urban context http://tinyurl.com/ ct6pebp) in the former communist, eastern part of the city and especially on the area around the Weitlingstraße, just south of the train station. This area is particularly infamous as a far-right hotspot in terms of election results, the number of propaganda offences and registered acts of far-right violence. The dubious reputation of this area known as Weitlingkiez is not a recent phenomenon. Already in the former GDR ('East Germany') far-right activists chose to settle in this area, which culminated in the squatting of a whole residential building and the establishment of several communal housing projects by neo-Nazis; the social and infrastructural seeds for the situation in the years to follow. For further details about the historical context see Luzar et al. (2006).

> Because of the (media) attention Lichtenberg receives, it is more fun (both for lefties and righties) to spray, gather etc. there. Lichtenberg is simply a good stage to be seen. In other words, the reputation attracts people even from outside. A self-reinforcing dynamic. (Interviewee Ber-11)

Some argue that the living conditions in the form of massive residential high-rises are partly to blame for the problem. The housing stock in the Weitlingkiez, however, consists mainly of three- to four-storey houses from the late nineteenth century, most of which have been renovated after the German reunification (street view http://tinyurl.com/btgmpd6). Our investigation shows that the range of artefacts, small and large, with a mirroring and mediating effect, did not differ much between such different types of residential settings, for example between the Weitlingstraße and Neu-Hohenschönhausen, an area dominated by large high-rise blocks with a similar reputation (street view http://tinyurl.com/cbly4nz).

SHOWING EXTREME-RIGHT PRESENCE

As alluded to above, far-right extremists are not in a position to shape the urban environment on a large scale. They typically have to rely on small interventions like affixing stickers to trash bins, posters to lamp posts or spraying graffiti. With the exception of some fences around a few private properties, most material interventions by far-right extremists have no direct effect on the human body.

Rather, they are typically based on the semantic content of certain messages or the semiotic quality of symbols.

In some cases, such as the NPD sticker shown in Figure 6.1, the message on the very top is very explicit and straightforward: 'Überfremdung stoppen!' (literally, 'Stop over-foreignisation'. A unique German expression meaning something like 'Stop the erosion of Germanness through the overwhelming presence of foreigners'). No decipherment is required to understand the intention of the author.

Figure 6.1
Sticker of the
right-wing
party NPD

> Posters and stickers come in waves, for example during anniversaries (of Rudolf Hess' death etc.). At the moment there are very few because posters and stickers are usually removed after one week. Even normal citizens help with this removal. (Interviewee Ber-25)

The situation is only slightly different for a swastika: Although its communicative content is not carried by words, its message is understood by everyone. This and other very explicit symbols are therefore illegal in Germany in the same way as it is a criminal act to publicly deny the Holocaust. The German law enforcement authorities therefore try to crack down on the public display of illegal symbols but cannot prevent their appearance in rare and even creative cases (Figure 6.2).

Many other public displays of the right-wing ideology and the presence of their proponents are much less direct and require a degree of de-coding. Their effect therefore depends upon the receiver's ability to read and decipher the textual or visual message. This makes such symbols hard to control, subject to different interpretations and intentionally elusive in legal terms. Such coded messages can therefore become somehow invisible to the gullible resident or visitor. However, to the initiated peer – and very often to the 'enemy' and potential victim – they speak loudly and clearly. The number 18, for example, sometimes stands for the first and eighth letter of the alphabet and thus represents the initials of Adolf Hitler. According to an analogous logic, the number 88 stands for 'Heil Hitler'. 'C4 for Reds' (Figure 6.3) is a call to kill political enemies on the left (reds) with a particular plastic explosive which is sold under the brand name C4.

Figure 6.2
Swastika in snow

Figure 6.3
Graffiti for the
initiated at an
underpass near
Lichtenberg
train station in
September 2008

Part of our project was a mental mapping exercise and photo-documentation with students from the Manfred von Ardenne Gymnasium in north Lichtenberg (coordinated by Christine Lasch). It revealed an appalling but fascinating variety of such messages in the form of graffiti and posters but mostly stickers and decals. While such aggressive displays of a self-proclaimed right-wing presence or the declaration of a 'racially pure' area might not in themselves do bodily harm or physically interfere with anyone's everyday life, their intimidating effect can be very real in a material and spatial sense nevertheless, for example by changing someone's commuting route. They are also intended to recruit followers and to tilt the discursive playing field, which would, if successful, shape the notion of what is considered normal and acceptable in public talk – if not in formal realms such as parliaments then at least in pubs.

> *The transport system is very sensitive to the graffiti issue: you'll find windows scratched and metro interiors tagged, but if it is rightwing extremist writing, it is removed very quickly – the rest instead can stay. (Interviewee Ber-32)*

As in every other case we studied, the symbolic and coded nature of certain urban artefacts brings with it the danger of paranoia and over-interpretation for a researcher. One insider of the Antifa scene, for example, assured us that a pub with the name 'Zapfhahn No. 88' (Figure 6.4) has nothing to do with neo-Nazis and their cryptic numerology but is just an ordinary pub for ordinary people.

Figure 6.4
Apparently just
an ordinary
pub despite its
suspicious name

But what does it signify if someone chooses to display 14 German flags in their backyard? This would not be worth mentioning during the football world championship in an ordinary, mid-size town; but the situation in Figure 6.5 is in the Weitlingstraße on a day when no national sports competition was taking place.

Figure 6.5
A sign of legitimate
national pride
or of chauvinist
patriotism?

A significant related problem is the voyeurism of the media, which searches and broadcasts the most drastic exemplars of far-right displays without providing nuanced context, thus further ruining the reputation of an area to the detriment of its citizens and retailers – and possibly to the benefit of the right-wing community.

FAR-RIGHT INFRASTRUCTURE

As mentioned above, the majority of artefacts that owe their existence to the struggle between far-right extremists and others are mainly of a symbolic nature; but not all. The purpose and effect of some does rest on their sheer materiality. This includes physical infrastructures like meeting points (Figure 6.6) and communal living projects (Wohngemeinschaften). The latter are typically rather inconspicuous from the outside because they are mainly rented flats within larger buildings (Figure 6.7).

Figure 6.6
Industrial area
at the Joseph
Orlopp Straße –
private property
of Berlin's former
NPD president and
alleged meeting
point for his party's
supporters

Figure 6.7
Nothing
conspicuous about
Weitlingstraße 80,
allegedly housing
a communal living
arrangement of
far-right activists

Retail outlets selling far-right paraphernalia are important too and can range widely in appearance (figures 6.8 and 6.9).

Figure 6.8
Supply of
right-wing
paraphernalia in
the Kategorie-C
store, Prerower-
Platz 1 – the
German Fraktur
Font is often
associated with
the Third Reich
(although it was
actually partly
banned by the
Nazis in 1941)

Figure 6.9
Tønsberg clothes
– very popular
among far-right
youths – are
available at the
Doorbreaker
store inside the
Linden-Center Mall

Also pubs are of special significance and many carry more or less telling names and symbols (Figure 6.10).

Figure 6.10
Far-right
infrastructure and
meeting point:
Pub 'Rumpelratz'
in the Joseph-
Orlopp-Straße. Just
opposite the area
seen in Figure 6.6.

Private properties are often used as places for strategic and entertainment meetings. A remarkable example is the building Wönnichstraße 1, which – certainly back in 2008 – belongs to a right-wing activist, was attacked by far-left aggressors and consequently remodelled into a fortress-like structure (Figure 6.11, street view at http://tinyurl.com/ckunvkz).

Figure 6.11
A fortified private
property and
meeting point of
far-right activists
after a paint
bomb attack

CPTED

While physical interventions in Berlin's urban fabric will never be able to eradicate far-right ideologies, they are still expected to at least contribute to the prevention of criminal acts committed in the name of such ideologies. Remarkably, the vast majority of crime scenes are publicly accessible spaces (Figure 6.12).

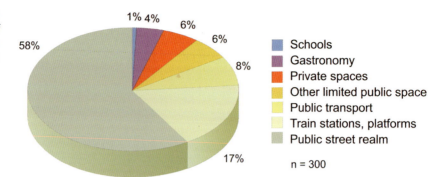

Figure 6.12 Spatial types of crime scenes 2003–6

Some things like railway lines act as de-facto demarcation lines – for example between the Weitlingkiez and Friedrichshain. They have a 'sorting' effect when people make residential location choices. (Interviewee Ber-10)

Many objects in Lichtenberg's public realm were therefore erected by official authorities according to the design principle of 'defensive architecture' or 'CPTED' (Crime Prevention Through Environmental Design). Their intention is to physically protect properties and human beings through their sheer material presence. For example, thorny bushes were deliberately planted in front of a pro-Nicaragua mural to thwart further smirch attacks on it (Figure 6.13).

The Kiezgarten (neighbourhood garden, Figure 6.14) just off Weitlingstraße is an example of another physical intervention related to CPTED rationales. It required sturdy fencing in order to turn it into the safe haven that it now is for children who used to feel intimidated on the public green space (Münsterlandplatz) just across the street by the aggressive breeds of dogs with which rough guys, often far-right extremists, prefer to display their ferocity.

Some other material interventions are not necessarily made to protect human beings but as an attempt to build resilience into artefacts against speech attacks. A classic example are gabions (strong wire baskets filled with stones) that replaced smooth concrete walls in some places in order to make the life of extremist graffiti sprayers impossible or at least harder (Figure 6.15) – with varying success.

Figure 6.13
Pro-Nicaragua
mural, protected
near the ground
with a row of
thorny bushes

Figure 6.14
A fortified safe
haven for children.
Street view
http://tinyurl.
com/7jrd49n.

Figure 6.15
Gabions near
Nöldnerplatz.
Street view
http://tinyurl.
com/bp568y2.

In many other cases, design decisions result from the attempt to protect potential victims of xenophobic aggression from potential perpetrators. Due to the previous frequency of assaults, mainly against non-native looking citizens by far-right extremists near the train station in Lichtenberg, its recent reconstruction incorporated a number of CPTED features such as CCTV cameras (Figure 6.16), extended sight-lines to facilitate human surveillance and an improved illumination scheme. The most visible deterrent is the permanent presence of a police van right outside the station (Figure 6.17).

Figure 6.16
Ubiquitous CCTV
at Lichtenberg
train station

Figure 6.17
Berlin Lichtenberg
station after
the recent
reconstruction

The portrayal (by the media) is that Friedrichshain (stronghold of some left-wing activists) and the Weitlingkiez (right-wing) are antagonists. Sometimes, right-wingers use the U5 connection (a specific underground line), go to Friedrichshain, chase some left youths and quickly withdraw with the U5. (Interviewee Ber-25)

Some criticise such measures as self-fulfilling prophecies because they allegedly signal the presence of danger and thus create an atmosphere of fear, even if it is more subjective than before. We tend to agree that CPTED can never be a panacea and must never be the only design guideline. Conversely, it is also clear that design that violates such principles can cause real problems. The spatial and material setting around the Linden Centre shopping mall (Figure 6.18) in North Lichtenberg, for example, ignores some basic CPTED ideas and is therefore perceived as dangerous by some potential victims of the far-right youths who tend to hang out here.

Figure 6.18
Linden Centre in
North Lichtenberg,
Prerower Platz

COUNTER-VOICES FROM THE CIVIL SOCIETY

The determination of the civil society to counter far-right extremists in their neighbourhood varies. Some are merely – but legitimately – concerned about the value of their property if it is located in a notorious area. Some realise that neo-Nazis are among their client base and should therefore not be disgruntled, which is part of the reason why the shopkeepers' association in one area could not agree on a campaign against violence from the right, but simply against violence in general.

Quite predictably, the Antifa scene chooses different means for its street-discourse strategy, namely graffiti, posters and stickers. Some of its more extreme sections also engage in more direct action as evidenced by the effects of a paint bomb attack visible in Figure 6.11. But also the middle of the civil society is very active and tries to 'speak up visually' against far-right extremism wherever they can. At the most basic level, ordinary citizens have started to routinely remove stickers with extremist content from lamp posts. In most cases, however, the counter-voices from the civil society are more or less loosely organised as some sort of club or initiative. These can even include rather ordinary and politically uncharged organisations. Lichtenberg's chess club, for example, presents itself on one of 10 'theme trees' (Themenbäume, Figure 6.19), which were provided with public money in an effort to foster 'social cohesion' (Planergemeinschaft 2008) in this neighbourhood. Theme trees are also part of the arsenal to counter Lichtenberg's reputation as source of constant bad news by demonstrating its ordinariness.

Figure 6.19
Theme tree along
Weitlingstraße/
Münsterlandplatz

A more direct engagement with far-right and anti-Semitic ideas are the 1,400 so-called 'stumbling stones' (Stolpersteine, www.stolpersteine.com, Figure 6.20), which can be found in the pavement in front of many houses throughout Berlin. They commemorate victims of the Third Reich, who used to live in these houses and whose names are engraved into the metal. This initiative is not unique to Berlin, however. Stumbling stones have been planted in over 500 German cities and some abroad. Still, their high number in Berlin is an explicit sign that counter-voices have not surrendered the street to right-wing raucous bawling. In other words, they demonstrate the presence of alternative discourses.

The local administration of the Bezirk Lichtenberg is also very active in countering the presence and visibility of far-right extremists in the area; especially since Christina Emmrich from the party Die Linke (The Left) was elected as Bezirk mayor in 2001. As a result, the extremely aggressive graffiti 'C4 for Reds', shown in Figure 6.3, has since been replaced by a mural celebrating diversity (Figure 6.21). In this sense, the civil society constantly attempts to take back the sovereignty over its urban space.

Figure 6.20
A stumbling stone
in Lichtenberg

Figure 6.21
The same wall
that once featured
'C4 for Reds'
(Figure 6.3); here
in mid-2009

A similar but temporary display of diversity was installed at the rear of a bus bay outside the Lichtenberg train station. It simply said 'I, too, am the city' and contained the enlarged signatures of children, many of which with clearly non-German names (Figure 6.22).

Figure 6.22
Making diversity
undeniable

Besides such relatively subtle and somewhat indirect ripostes some others tackle far-right extremism head-on and engage in frontal cognitive altercation. Figure 6.23, for example, shows a container with the slogan 'The middle against the right', a play on words because this initiative is spearheaded by the central borough of Berlin (Mitte = centre) Its opposite side features several posters which unpick and vitiate common false arguments and biased interpretations of the far-right discourse. Several of such containers have been placed on key sites, mainly in the centre of Berlin. Interestingly, the one shown here is located in front of a Tønsberg store, a brand of clothes ill-famed as neo-Nazi street gear. A left-wing attack with paint bombs explains the red spots over and next to the window.

Figure 6.23
Setting the facts
straight – not
in a book but
on the street

While all of these efforts are clearly somehow political, some other initiatives aim to emphasise the importance of the Political realm (note the capital P) in the sense of parliaments and formal decision-making bodies. Figure 6.24 shows such an attempt: A sticker urging the reader 'No vote for Nazis'.

Figure 6.24
Dragging the
controversy back
to the (capital
P) Political

FACILITATING CIVILITY

Not all artefacts and material interventions that owe their shape – at least to some degree – to the real and reputed presence of right-wing extremists are negative, against the undesired and trying to prevent or confront a problem. A different category of measures aspires to prompt positive alternatives, to enable desired behaviours and to facilitate civility in the sense of a civilised society. Facilities that allow harmless distraction belong to this group, especially where they are targeted toward that social group, which is assumed to be most susceptible to right-wing ideologies: young under-challenged males, who might otherwise translate their boredom into some mischief. A typical example is the skater park near the Lichtenberg railway station and (by coincidence?) directly opposite the fortified property of far-right activists shown in Figure 6.11, which is on the far left of Figure 6.25 (urban context at http://tinyurl.com/crmlbo9).

Even more ambitious are the attempts to facilitate not only harmless activities but friendly encounters between people of different ethnic, cultural, religious and linguistic backgrounds in a convenient environment. A number of Multi-cultural Centres belong to this category as well as, very prominently, Inter-cultural Gardens (Figure 6.26).

Figure 6.25
Skater park near
Lichtenberg
train station

Figure 6.26
Inter-cultural
Garden,
Lichtenberg

The 'Foundation Inter-culture' (Stiftung Interkultur) helped to initiate 24 of these gardens in different parts of Berlin to provide opportunities for their users to 'discover their shared human nature in conversations over last night's slug attack' as one interviewee put it. Unsurprisingly, such facilities are objects of political scrutiny by far-right politicians, who paid an official visit to Lichtenberg's Inter-cultural Gardens shortly after our visit in order to inspect whether public money has been properly invested for such a 'suspicious' mix of beneficiaries. Unfortunately, some of these gardens are also targets of graffiti and even arson attacks. As can be seen in Figure 6.27, sometimes quite creative forms of material resilience can be found: After several graffiti attacks, it was covered with vine whose leaves make an extremely unsuitable surface for graffiti sprayers.

Figure 6.27
The shed in the
Inter-cultural
Garden Lichtenberg
with herbal
resilience

7

The Amsterdam Case

Amsterdam is frequently portrayed as a city of tolerance (Figure 7.1). Popular accounts explain this with Amsterdam's long-standing tradition as a city of co-existence between different cultural, ethnic and religious groups, and of merchants focused on profit rather than on differences of origin, language or religion. Inter-group violence and tension in recent decades have been rare: '[t]here have not been riots like those in Paris or Bradford, and there have not been violent confrontations with extreme-right groups like there have been in Germany' (Veldhuis and Bakker 2009: 107). Lately, however, the city's famous *gedogen* (toleration) principle has come under the pressure of phenomena of radicalisation and debates about the integration of the country's Muslim communities.

Figure 7.1
The urban and civic identity of Amsterdam as a free and open city requires constant reproduction, including through material interventions like this commemoration stone

Like in many other cities, the 9/11 attacks against New York and the Pentagon and the subsequent War on Terror left their mark on Amsterdam's urban security policies. The assassinations of the politician Pim Fortuyn in 2002 and of film director Theo Van Gogh in 2004 (Figure 7.2) – both outspoken critics of Islam – made these processes even more relevant. These events seem to be symptoms of a larger radicalisation trend on the right-wing extreme of the political spectrum as well as among Muslim citizens of the Netherlands.

Figure 7.2 Statue in Amsterdam's Oosterpark commemorating film director and Islam critic Theo Van Gogh, murdered in 2004 by Mohammed Bouyeri, a Dutch-Muslim extremist who grew up in the neighbourhood of Slotervaart

Research conducted after these events mainly focused on the radicalisation of young Muslims and showed that many of them experience alienation both from their first-generation immigrant parents and from the Dutch society. A well-known study by Buijs et al. (2006) concluded that the majority of Muslim youths seek integration into the Dutch society, but are not readily admitted, which triggers frustration along a broad escalation spectrum all the way towards radicalisation – primarily among Turkish youths. Experts argue that 2 per cent of Amsterdam Muslims are 'potentially the most receptive to radicalisation' (Slootman and Tillie 2006: 4). And although this figure and underlying definitions are subject to dispute, radicalisation – especially Muslim radicalisation – scores high on the Dutch security policy agenda. In 2007, the Dutch government dedicated eight million euros to prevent radicalisation (Municipality of Amsterdam 2007). Although it briefly refers to right-wing and animal rights extremism, the 2011 Dutch National Counter-terrorism Strategy defines radicalisation as an overwhelmingly Islamic phenomenon, as 'the process of a growing internalisation of a way of thinking inspired by al Qaeda' (Ministry of Security and Justice 2011: 69). Unsurprisingly, therefore, young Muslims are the prime target of the Dutch state radicalisation prevention policy. If radicalisation is perceived as such a pressing problem, what is the role of Amsterdam's urban environment in reflecting and shaping the issues that are potentially at its basis – such as failed integration and polarisation between population groups?

THE CASE STUDY

Our project focused on the neighbourhood of Slotervaart in the west of the Amsterdam conurbation. Here, the *gedogen* principle has come particularly under pressure. Slotervaart is the first area in the Netherlands to have developed – upon the initiative of its own Muslim mayor – anti-radicalisation and zero-tolerance policies to tackle anti-social behaviour among its young residents. The area, with 44,000 inhabitants of which about 11,000 are Muslim (Bartels and De Jong 2008), is considered at high risk because of its ethnic composition, segregation along ethnic/religious lines and institutional affiliation to different places of worship, and previous ethnically charged riots. It is also the area where Theo Van Gogh's murderer – the Dutch-Muslim Mohammad Bouyeri – grew up. This context prompted the development of the 'Slotervaart Action Plan: Countering Radicalisation' (2007).

Slotervaart is characterised by many modern high-rise blocks and separated from inner Amsterdam by the Rembrandt Park and the motorway A10 (http://goo.gl/maps/Q1KBs). These are often perceived as infrastructural boundaries that are difficult and occasionally unsafe to access let alone cross for some, thus creating a sense of being cut off from the rest of the city (Figure 7.3).

Figure 7.3 Rembrandt Park is theoretically Slotervaart's main green asset, but only accessible through tunnels under a six-lane highway. Black seems the paint of choice due to its maximum opacity which allows to easily paint over graffiti.

Figure 7.4 Housing near August Allebéplein, Slotervaart's main square

At least two interrelated socio-material processes are noteworthy in the history of Slotervaart: firstly, a massive wave of residential construction to provide larger, lighter, healthier living conditions in the suburbs for the Dutch population after the Second World War (Figure 7.4). Secondly, a wave of immigration consisting mainly of workers from Turkey and Morocco, that followed immigrants from the former Dutch colonies such as the Dutch Antilles and Indonesia. These large post-war residential schemes were originally built for Dutch families. However, with time their population became more ethnically diverse as an increasing number of Dutch moved out and immigrant families moved in.

Complex socio-economic factors related to these waves of immigration have triggered segregation processes with the effect that many Turks and Moroccans today live in the west of the city (Musterd and Ostendorf 1998). As maps 7.1 and 7.2 illustrate, the percentage of population of Turkish or Moroccan background often coincides with social housing dwellings and is clearly concentrated in the western suburbs such as Slotervaart. For the Planning Department of the City of Amsterdam, these maps prove that 'ethnical tensions in the city relate more to social and income status and spatial concentration of groups, rather than to cultural discourses about ethnic origin' (Conversation with Planning Department of the City of Amsterdam, 2 August 2012). The Dutch government is committed to tackling segregation and some of its measures are already visible in everyday urban life, for example the recent ban of some forms of veiling for women (such as the burqa and the niqab) in public.

The following pages illustrate three urban polarisation processes in Slotervaart related to youth, cultural difference (including religion) and security. The built environment has clear implications in all these processes: in the way it mirrors social relationships of inequality and distrust (as well as positive contact) and in the way it functions as agent for the improvement or worsening of these relationships.

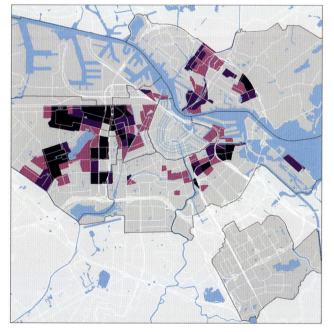

Turkey – Marocco
percentage of citizens
■ 30% or more
■ 20% to 30%
■ 10% to 20%

Gemeente Amsterdam
Dienst Ruimtelijke Ordening

GIS-loket - september 2006

Map 7.1
Percentage of
Turkish and
Moroccan citizens
in Amsterdam

Map 7.2
Percentage of
social housing
dwellings in
Amsterdam

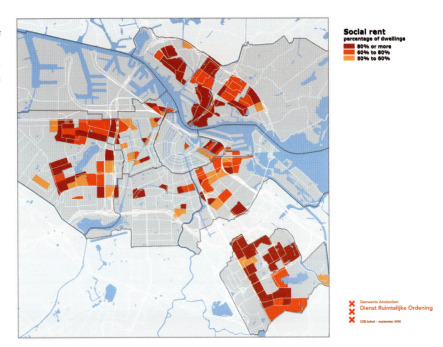

HANGPLEKKEN

An interesting material phenomenon in Amsterdam – and Slotervaart is no exception to that – are the so-called *hangplekken* (hang-out places). Frequently found near squares, playing grounds, or specific street corners, these potentially convivial spaces are perceived by some – often older Dutch people – as threatening when frequented by youngsters, many of whom happen to be unemployed and of a non-Dutch ethnic background. Hangplekken are often portrayed in a rather simplified version as 'dangerous', 'dominated' by Muslims, or even as places of recruitment into radical activist circles. And indeed, numerous instances of rather defensive architecture have been observed in and around these hang-out spots, possibly in response to – or as pre-emptive measures against – acts of vandalism.

Some interviewees related such (real and perceived) anti-social behaviours to the lack of physical infrastructures for harmless alternative activities: community centres, rooms for after-school activities, sports facilities on the one hand and attractive private residential space on the other. The latter problem allegedly is accentuated by the size of many flats which were originally built for average four-member Dutch nuclear families but are easily outgrown by immigrant families who tend to have more children: 'it is not uncommon to see eight-member families living in cramped, 50-square-meter (540-square-foot) apartments' (Wiedemann 2007). Adolescents with an immigrant background thus have a material incentive to spend their time on the street. This, again, feeds into stereotypes and fears linked to hangplekken, complicating the friendly co-existence of different ethnicities and ratcheting dynamics of polarisation and mutual mistrust.

Figure 7.5 Mercator Square (Mercatorplein) in Slotervaart

Let us take the example of Mercator Square (Figure 7.5). Built in 1925, the square was redesigned in 1998 at great expense, but failed to attract a vibrant street life for everyone and is considered by many as still in a phase of transition.

Mercatorplein is claimed as 'hang-out place' by young people – many of non-Dutch background – whom some perceive as threatening. Apparently, the consumption of drugs there has become such a problem that the authorities resorted to high degrees of creativity (Figure 7.6) to regulate alcohol and drug-related practices.

Figure 7.6
Regulating 'hangplekken' on Mercatorplein

Figure 7.7
Due to the inevitable flexibility of appropriation of any material intervention, no one can completely control whether these tables in August Allebéplein are actually used for chess games or as 'hangplekken'

Hangplekken are the material expression of the fine line existing between providing planned spaces that facilitate conviviality by attracting ordinary, law-abiding people into the public realm (such as at the August Allebéplein chessboards in Figure 7.7), and the only partly controllable appropriation of their use as 'hang-out' infrastructures, and occasionally as targets of vandalism.

CULTURAL DIFFERENCE, RELIGION AND PUBLIC SPACE

In Slotervaart, the construction of mosques is a particularly contested issue. Some inhabitants, especially older native Dutch, perceive their existence and the changes that mosques bring to the everyday built environment as a sign of encroachment of Islam into the Dutch society. Others criticise certain architectural design features (especially the minarets) as statement of alleged religious imposition over a predominantly secular society. In some cases, however, Amsterdam's new mosques have produced – at least at the design stage – compromises between Islam and Dutch native culture, such as in the case of the Western Mosque (Figure 7.8). The Western Mosque was planned as a centre for prayer, but also for a range of more profane uses at Baarsjesweg (about 500 metres east of Rembrandt Park). Although initiated by Muslims, it was intended as asset for the wider neighbourhood, and was designed according to the architectural norms of the Amsterdam School.[1] For a variety of reason spanning from opposition of local groups to problems with its developer, the project was halted.

> Churches are being demolished because they aren't used enough any longer by the local population … It is hard to get used to that change, when three mosques are built here in Slotervaart, and not a church. Where you used to have a Dutch bakery, there is now a Moroccan bakery with an Arabic name. (Interviewee Ams-52)

Clearly, these perceptions are not supported by systematic empirical evidence, however it is apparent how different cultural and religious practices rub against each other very closely in Slotervaart's everyday urban environment, such as the alcohol retail outlet in Figure 7.9.

---

1   The Amsterdam School is an architectural style that rose in the Netherlands between 1910 and 1930 and was applied to the design of public institutions and schools, as well as working-class housing. Its main features were brick construction with elaborate building schemes together with ornate masonry, sculpture, glass- and ironwork.

Figure 7.8
The site of the
Westermoskee
in Amsterdam

Figure 7.9
Alcohol is available
until late in the
evening from this
store at the August
Allebéplein, just
two buildings
away from a
mosque

The space around mosques is another matter of concern. Perhaps the most blatant case is that of a police station built next to the mosque on August Allebéplein (Figure 7.10). For some people, this is a blunt form of state control and surveillance over the Muslim community. For the police members whom we spoke with, however, this proximity is both a mere result of availability of space and – if anything – a sign of partnership. Again, we cannot over-interpret rumours and individual opinions. What we can materially observe, however, is how its defensive architecture and surveillance cameras overlook the mosque's outdoor praying area (Figure 7.11) in a way that, for some, might do very little to transmit the sense of partnership and good neighbourliness expressed to us by a local police officer.

Figure 7.10
August Allebéplein: Mosque and police station, the latter built after the former

Figure 7.11
On a sunny Friday, worshippers exceeding the capacity of the modest mosque spill out onto the small public space with extra carpets, overlooked by the police station

> *We should be careful not to over-interpret that fact that there is a police station next to the mosque at the August Allebéplein. It might be that this police station was built before Theo van Gogh's assassination, maybe even before the riots. (Interviewee Ams-13)*

The line between paranoia, surveillance, safety, stereotypes, (over-)interpretation and co-existence is also blurred by seemingly mundane artefacts as satellite dishes. The former are often taken by Dutch people as evidence of the presence of immigrants watching programmes broadcast in their country or region of origin (Figure 7.12). According to a local architect there is a different interpretation of private and 'home' space between the native Dutch and immigrant-background population, which produces a discrepancy between Dutch housing design and immigrant expectations:

> *[In the 1960s, Dutch] architects designed houses with large windows. That's a very Calvinistic thing: the street side of a house is the open side, the back side is for private issues. The same pattern prevails in the traditional inner city houses: the private rooms are in the back, whereas meeting rooms, etc. are in the front. The big windows, however, did not at all appeal to immigrants. When they moved in, they immediately covered the big windows with paper – even before they had the time to buy curtains. (Interviewee Ams-41)*

Banal types of artefacts such as these can, in an ethnically mixed neighbourhood, trigger (mis-)interpretations. Some interviewees highlighted the possibility that the presence of ornate net curtains (Figure 7.13) as opposed to the Dutch 'open windows tradition' (interviewee Ams-16), may be interpreted by certain portions of the native Dutch population as the residents' 'attempt to hide something'. This, associated with the presence of residents of immigrant background, can contribute to build a climate of suspicion between communities. One of our participatory photography project respondents in Slotervaart raised the issue of suspicion of resistance to integration (of the immigrant population).

> *You can see that there are many people living here that want to have television channels from Morocco, Turkey or for instance Egypt. [The number of satellite dishes] strengthens the feeling that only not-integrated foreigners are living in Overtoomse Veld. Therefore the area keeps its image of a "black" neighbourhood. (Participatory photography activity member)*

Although there is no empirical evidence that this is the case, what is important here is how certain elements of the built environment – even banal artefacts that are part of daily urban life – can stir up negative feelings, rumours, misinterpretation and potentially tension between communities.

Figure 7.12 Material mirrors of cultural difference in Slotervaart. Balconies on a block of flats display numerous satellite dishes, often used by families of Moroccan and Turkish background to watch programmes broadcast in their original homelands or in the wider Middle East. Another balcony instead displays a windmill, a national symbol of the Netherlands.

Figure 7.13 Different interpretations of private and home space in Slotervaart. In the same building, some windows are screened by net curtains, while others keep a degree of transparency by only adding some plants on the windowsill – very frequently a Dutch practice.

DEFENSIVE ARCHITECTURES

Polarisation between two poles can, in principle, always be caused by the distancing of both poles from each other. The way in which the built environment triggers negative feelings towards certain communities and their alleged 'lack of integration' shows that Slotervaart is experiencing what could be described as *relative* polarisation. In the context at hand, the immigrant community is not necessarily the only one that isolates and builds extremist views against the native Dutch. The latter might simultaneously erect a very similar kind of segregated mentality.

Figure 7.14 Who is 'us' and who is 'them'? Polarisation and radicalisation are relative phenomena. Who can say which pole increases the distance from the other(s)? Who would deny that Geert Wilders, leader of the Dutch far-right Party for Freedom, is one of the distancing poles?

In the built environment, this is mirrored in gated communities, defensible new architectures, hardening of infrastructure and increased surveillance. Slotervaart, too, has its share of such gated compounds (Figure 7.15). Many of them are linked to the wider process of neoliberal urban renewal which is resulting in new, commodified and privately owned developments for a higher income population.

By contrast, in other renewal projects like the one illustrated in Figure 7.16 much attention is paid to maintaining the existing population in place, and also – interestingly – to the egalitarian provision of infrastructure and the creation of better connections between private and public spaces. These projects are often run by the local city council and involve a substantial degree of residents' participation. Public input concerns not only the urban architecture, but also the interior design in ways that take into account the lifestyle of different communities.

Figure 7.15 A new gated development in Slotervaart for the better off, circled by thick metal fences and bricks that hinder transparency and interaction. For those inside this defensive design might imply the existence of an external threat. What feelings could such a landscape trigger for those outside?

Nowadays, some housing corporations attempt to redesign the interior of flats with input of the residents (mostly women). Moroccan residents often request to replace the corridor system (one corridor from which separate rooms are accessible) with a design that creates a communal central area for the whole family. (Interviewee Ams-8)

This is a very important aspect, especially when we consider that among the reasons for the proliferation of hangplekken in Slotervaart, is – as pointed out above – a lack of infrastructure for constructive activities for young people. This lack of infrastructure, as we noted, starts from the very design of the home, even before the lack of public infrastructure.

In other cases, however, urban renewal has provoked the displacement of many families (especially of immigrant background), as well as deepening the socio-economic gaps between neighbouring populations. Despite attempts by the local administration to improve the look of public spaces so to avoid or mitigate perceptions and feelings of inequality and envy, the wider process of urban renewal – with its consequent displacement and incoming new (wealthier) population – is adding a layer of polarising dynamics to the existing tensions. Existing polarisation and mistrust on one side, and deepening inequality, widespread security and surveillance and defensive architecture on the other, all nurture the socio-technical processes of polarisation in Slotervaart.

Figure 7.16
A renovation project in Derkinderenstraat in Slotervaart. Rather differently from the one in Figure 7.15, human activity and collective surveillance are brought onto the street by design. The previous design had only storage at the ground floor, but the renovation includes ground floor use for shops, offices and other activities.

> There is too little connection between science and decision-makers, councils, politicians. They have other goals. The goals of housing corporations is to keep the value of property as high as possible. However, they are beginning to shift and realise these dynamics. [In] Amsterdam, urban renewal is not organised very well … Yes, there is a vision about the buildings, the infrastructures and the economy of the future. But there is no vision of the society of the future. Buildings, infrastructures, the economy should be only instruments to achieve a good society, but they have mutated to ends in themselves. (Interviewee Ams-40)

The example of Diamond Square reflects well the potential ratcheting of mistrust fed by the built environment, such as surveillance infrastructure. A violent incident with an ethnic undertone took place at Diamond Square. Today, multiple CCTV cameras and very high fences are seen to protect spaces as small as private yards (Figure 7.17). The degree of defensive architecture includes fortified fencing, concrete bollards and window iron grids. The place breathes distrust and fear.

Once installed, however, it seems as if these 'distrustful' features signal a certain expectation in terms of what kind of clientele will frequent the square, thus perpetuating a cycle of mistrust based on the alleged reputation of the place. A similar dynamic has been highlighted by another of our participatory photography activity members while describing the security infrastructure at the nearby Piet Mondriaanplein square:

> Right in front of me is a pole with a camera placed on top probably to keep an eye on the youth that is hanging around here … Maybe people feel safer having the cameras around. But because of the cameras they also are aware of the fact that this area is known as an unsafe area. (Participatory camera activity member)

Figure 7.17
The material
setting of
Diamond Square
responds to social
conditions. As a
result, multiple
CCTV cameras
and a high fence
protect a local
community centre.

The built environment, in this sense, might start as a response to what is perceived as a social threat, but in some parts of Amsterdam, it risks turning into a socio-technical self-fulfilling prophecy.

8

Implications for Planning Practice and Policy

Most scholars working in the field of conflict and cities have made excellent attempts to communicate their findings in applicable ways to practitioners of all sorts (Bollens 2012; Calame and Charlesworth 2009; Dumper and Pullan 2010; Gaffikin and Morrissey 2011; Weizman 2007). With our particular angle on related issues we also felt the need and the responsibility to digest our findings in a similar way in order to make a real difference. For this reason, we produced a 'Charter for Spaces of Positive Encounters', which has become part of the touring exhibition that concluded the project. The charter is available on the website www.urbanpolarisation.org and consists of 21 brief 'findings in a nutshell' for practitioners, academics, policy-makers and various other social actors. This chapter draws on and elaborates the Charter and highlights the applicability and significance of the project findings for policy-makers and planning practitioners. Although key lessons are primarily spelled out for the UK context, we expect that most of them can also serve as a source of inspiration for other contexts as well.

THE PROJECT AND *PREVENT*

The third round of the ESCR/AHRC/FCO programme 'New Security Challenges' was specifically aimed to gather critical insight on phenomena of radicalisation and violence. This focus is informed by the cross-departmental government document CONTEST: *Countering International Terrorism: The United Kingdom's Strategy* presented in parliament in 2006 as part of a £3.5 billion reform of national security strategies and operative structures, which was originally launched in 2001.

Much has been written about building-in resilience into urban environments to face emergency (Adey and Anderson 2012; Coaffee and O'Hare 2008; Coaffee et al. 2008; Graham 2010). This literature on risk, resilience and material rigidity enrols the built environment in efforts to prepare the nation for a future of ubiquitous and continuous terrorist threats.

In an admittedly simplified nutshell one could argue that a lot of this literature focuses on a situation of an already existing threat whereas we tried join the ranks of those few people who look a bit upstream in the causal chain *before* or at least *while* situations deteriorate. This sits well with one of four strands within the UK's counter-terrorism strategy. The three strands which we leave to other colleagues are *Pursue, Prepare* and *Protect.* The fourth one, with which we identify much more, is the so-called *Prevent* strand. Only very few scholars have previously explored the role of the built environment for this theme. Hence our second research question: *'Are certain design features of cities (buildings, infrastructures, public spaces, etc.) particularly conducive to the generation and acceleration of different forms of polarisation?'* The *Prevent* strand, which was launched in 2007 and reviewed in 2011 under the coalition government, aims to develop preventive measures to tackle the conditions of radicalisation and foreclose the emergence of violent extremism, both in the UK and abroad – when this is perceived as a threat to the UK. It is premised upon the idea that a shift towards social cohesion and integration as complements to counter-terrorism measures such as surveillance and target hardening, is preferable or should at least supplement classic policing, because 'cohesive, empowered and resilient communities are best equipped to confront violent extremists and support the most vulnerable individuals. Violent extremists are able to gain a foothold where they are not effectively challenged' (HM Government 2008: 7). This principle produces a specific geography of 'vulnerable spaces', as 'Radicalisation towards active support for violent extremism is most likely to occur where extremists can act uncontested, away from mainstream voices and competing ideas. This can apply both to physical places – prisons, universities, mosques – and to virtual spaces on the internet' (HM Government 2008: 5). In response, *Prevent* has also engaged with local partners (for example through the Preventing Violent Extremism Pathfinder Fund) to allow young people to contribute to policy-making processes in the areas where they live or to create 'safe spaces for individuals and groups to discuss and work through difficult and emotive issues' (HM Government 2008: 8).

MATERIALISING *PREVENT*:
THE BUILT ENVIRONMENT AS MIRROR AND MEDIATOR OF POLARISATION

As mentioned previously, we soon grew unsatisfied with the term 'radicalisation'. This implies the movement and withdrawal of one group away from some accepted or at least mainstream position. It is therefore inevitably a judgemental term towards the individuals or groups seen as 'divergent'. *Polarisation*, however, describes a more relative phenomenon of mutual distancing which does not pre-answer the question which one of two (or more) poles moves away from the other; and which is the 'wrong' direction. Societal polarisation can be a typical precursor of radicalisation and violent extremism – after all, isolation and distance from mainstream voices is a key term in the Government's Preventing Violent Extremism Pathfinder fund (Department for Communities and Local Government 2007). Under this assumption, it is important to tackle polarisation as one of many ingredients of radicalisation.

If it is true that tangible elements of a city can have an influence not only on rather mundane aspects of people's life, but even on the process, practice and speed of polarisation itself, then it is reasonable to assume that careful planning interventions in the urban environment can contribute in some ways to prevent the deterioration or contribute to the improvement of such situations. This is not an outgrowth of social engineering or material determinism, but an acknowledgement that the scope for human agency is circumscribed by both social contingency and structural context. In other words, we see the urban environment not as the only factor determining the course of polarisation processes but at least as one of which there are many. Of course, we cannot simply knock down a fence and hope people will automatically start liking each other. But likewise, we cannot simply preach neighbourliness between warring social groups when a wall literally prevents visual and acoustic encounters. We therefore also focused on spatial and physical measures that could induce positive dynamics for peaceful encounters and possibly even de-polarisation and cohesion building. We developed a series of guidelines and suggestions to foster a more nuanced understanding of the interconnections between societal division and the built environment and to put this understanding to good use – but also to manage the expectations of those who might think we can design our way out of societal conflict. In essence, this is an attempt to contribute to the praxis of preventing polarisation and even perhaps radicalisation.

These suggestions, presented below, pull together the key points of various project outputs, including a submission to a parliamentary call for evidence about *Prevent* launched by the Communities and Local Government Committee on 21 July 2009 (Communities and Local Government Committee 2009); a presentation at the 2011 Counter-Terror Expo in London and a said 'Charter for Spaces of Positive Encounters' elaborated following the fieldwork research in all four case study cities. The latter was also discussed, tested and refined with 16 representatives of all four case cities during a workshop we held at the University of Manchester on 21 and 22 May 2009.

THE BUILT ENVIRONMENT AS MIRROR OF POLARISATION

Caution is necessary when trying to interpret the urban environment as seismograph of underlying but invisible polarisation trends in a given community. The attempt to 'read' urban artefacts as indicators of radicalisation/polarisation is tantamount to reverse engineering and comes with the typical danger of taking the wrong turn, because material conditions can have multiple causes. Like all urban artefacts, those that owe their existence or shape to some kind of polarisation trend have no essence, no single 'correct' significance or fixed place in this connection. Polarised built environments are more than 'texts' where researchers, policy-makers or professionals can simply 'read' cues of polarisation. Quite the opposite, they are shaped in complex ways by the micro-geographies of the neighbourhood, the street, the wider city and so on. What matters is the constellation of material and social conditions. Their interpretation requires detailed knowledge of the local context and subtleties. With the exception of emblematic divided cities like Beirut or Belfast, polarisation is rarely apparent to the untrained eye and radicalised individuals or groups would hardly make themselves ostentatiously visible. While this interpretations might reveal a better understanding for 'outsiders', those who already possess sufficient local knowledge often do not glean much new information from this type of investigation beyond what they already know.

Dominant policy and media discourses (including the Preventing Violent Extremism Pathfinder programme) tend to seek and locate polarising trends within non-mainstream, isolated (and isolating) groups that drift away from the mainstream of society. Further research has refuted this argument, showing that radicalisation is more likely to trigger from within mainstream environments than in 'already-radicalised' or 'isolated' ones (Hoskins et al. 2011). This is often because of grievances triggered or worsened by dominant discourses on multiculturalism or foreign policy, for example. Our research, however, shows that polarisation is often characterised by the drifting apart of two or more poles from each other: polarisation is thus relational. The mainstream pole can sometimes drift away from minority or disadvantaged groups as well and this can have material consequences too. One example are fortress-style developments of the majority's middle class, that are exclusive, gated, segregated and could even reinforce grievances and feelings of inequality among certain groups, as seen in the urban restructuring programmes of Amsterdam's peripheries.

At certain stages of escalation, radicalising groups seem to prefer different degrees of visibility for different audiences, for example rallying support within one's own community versus deceiving authorities and opponents. There are two important points to make here, especially in the context of how *Prevent* – and its related counter-terrorism hotline run by the London's Metropolitan Police Service – are tagging certain artefacts and spaces as suspicious. Firstly, covert (potentially violent) action, is probably not the only motivation for the material and/or spatial decisions of radicalised groups or individuals. This is particularly valid when the public is asked to 'keep an eye' on certain locations deemed as gathering points to prepare violent action. The initiative 'Safer Runnymede', near Sara's former workplace, contains a special section on preventing violent extremism, which asks the public to notice potential suspicious activity especially as 'Extremist groups meet … at community centres'. We feel it is extremely important not to stigmatise portions of the built environment – such as community centres – without differentiating between licit activity, non-violent extremism and violent extremism. This leads to our second point: The assumption that any spatial or material ambiguity indicates illicitness can backfire. This is the case of certain counter-terrorism awareness initiatives like the posters and leaflets produced for the Metropolitan Police Service anti-terrorist hotline. One of these leaflets, for example, points at an unnamed doorbell as an alleged indicator of illicit activities (http://content.met.police.uk/Campaign/counterterrorism2011). Drawing attention to the ambiguity or even potential danger of everyday artefacts is, on the one hand, a way to alert communities to the possible presence of terrorists within everyday environments; on the other hand, however, it can stigmatise practices, places and objects as banal as a doorbell. It does not take long to conclude that this is an openly simplistic and potentially counter-productive assumption about certain features of the built environment as indicators of radicalisation. The Metropolitan Police is also providing a list of artefacts (without specifying any criteria of selection) that are classified as 'suspicious', which amounts to a blanket demonisation of those artefacts and their combinations with particular behaviours. But in most cases they are simply ordinary parts of the cities we live in and their singling-out thus creates even more suspicion, even less mutual trust and perhaps even less cohesion. According to London's Metropolitan Police, the following practices are deemed suspicious: 'excessive van rental'; 'large quantities' of mobile phones; use of cameras; presence of masks and goggles 'dumped somewhere'; computers, suitcases and people travelling and 'being vague about where they are going'; 'padlocks, lock-ups, garages and sheds' (see also the image of the shed at http://tinyurl.com/9e5puoq) and 'anyone renting a commercial property' (Metropolitan Police 2012). Other artefacts include: bins, containers, doorbells, refund vouchers and credit card transactions receipts. Besides being potentially counter-productive, similar initiatives might drive radicalised individuals to higher levels of professionalism. We call for less essentialist, more nuanced and more contextualised approaches by policy-makers towards the potential presence and detection of radicalisation that are attentive to local specificities. This is of particular importance when the denunciation of ambiguous artefacts stigmatises certain areas, activities and objects for a long time. A more 'front-line' approach based on community police officers who liaise with the community and know the specific context seems a more productive and certainly less damaging strategy rather than delegating these tasks to public judgement on the basis of vague guidelines and a phone line.

Symbols are of particular importance in polarising/radicalising situations. While it is important to suppress the use of outright inflammatory symbols – where possible – attention must be paid to potential side-effects. A tough approach to the display of symbols and logos, for example of particular illegal groups or specific worldviews, can lead to a game-like series of attempts to outsmart the other side. Our findings in Berlin are a clear case of this phenomenon where the fact that the display of certain symbols like the swastika is illegal has led to more and more cryptic communication strategies of far-right extremists in the urban fabric. Xenophobic, inflammatory, anti-Semitic or other message are nowadays encoded in statements like 'C4 for Reds' (see Figure 6.3). Also a more or less sophisticated numerology is used to mark far-right infrastructures (see Chapter 6 for examples). This coding and de-coding process can even create a degree of fun and excitement and thus increase the attractiveness of becoming or at least of remaining an insider.

THE BUILT ENVIRONMENT AS MEDIATOR OF POLARISATION

When we talk about the urban environment as a mediator of polarisation we refer to the notion that space, buildings and other material phenomena are not just simply passive, harmless and therefore innocent containers within which social activities are played out. We think, and found evidence for this, that the urban environment has a degree of agency and should be understood as some kind of actor. Obviously not with an independent, innate will and intentions to pursue certain goals, but with certain consequences upon the social. While many of these may be unintended side-effects, a large number of them are deliberately built-into them by those human actors who designed, financed, constructed and maintain them. We do not adhere to any form of material determinism. We do not believe that there is a mono-causal link between a certain material/spatial setting and the social consequences. Our world is far too complex – and fascinating – for such simple mechanisms. We are convinced, however, that materiality is one of many factors that co-shape our social reality. In other words, it mediates the social.

'The material' and 'the social' are clearly too abstract and too highly aggregated terms. In order to do justice to the complexity of polarisation as a socio-material phenomenon we thus need a more nuanced view of the underlying processes and parameters. We suggest the following differentiation of built environment related factors: those related to the process of becoming radical and those related to the behaviour of already radicals.

Table 8.1 Social and spatial aspects in the context of radicalis*ing* and
radicalis*ed* individuals and groups

Becoming radical	segregation	'isolation hypothesis', the assumption that a lack of exposure to 'otherness' leads to polarisation, stereotypisation, in some cases even to radicalisation
	grievances	esp. local level, neighbourhood
	ideological fuel	spaces (literal and virtual) and the city as message board
	recruitment	spaces (literal and virtual)
Behaviour of radicals	meeting points	strategic infrastructure
	targets/victims	number, ease of attack/escape

The rubric 'becoming radical' is only relevant in the context of home-grown radicalisation. The rubric 'behaviour of radicals' is relevant for the operation area of extremists, regardless of where they became radicalised.

Our various conversations with sociologists, psychologists and political scientists indicates that there is wide consensus that segregation, grievances (global as well as local), ideological inflammation and certain recruitment conditions are not sufficient conditions of radicalisation. It is often difficult even to isolate any necessary conditions for radicalisation. All these factors, can, however, contribute to the process, possibly in a cumulative way. Our research has shown that the built environment can alleviate or accentuate these conditions. In other words, if material interventions cannot stop radicalisation, this does not mean they are irrelevant. Relatedly, what seem like unrelated or banal built environment interventions (such as road construction, road diversions, the upgrade of public places and urban renewal) can have unintended knock-on effects for polarisation/radicalisation trends, as we have shown with processes of urban renewal in Amsterdam.

Artefacts have no 'ultimately true' essence – rather, their meaning and effect is always dependent on the beholder. It is difficult, therefore, to predict the effects of this kind of everyday built environment interventions, both planned or otherwise. Their appropriation depends on local practices, power dynamics, representation by the media, existing socio-economic contexts, and so on. This implies a call for the devolution of responsibility for built environment-related interventions to lower levels of the spatial hierarchy because this is where, by definition, local knowledge sits. In other words, interventions need to be planned and discussed in neighbourhood X rather than in Whitehall. This does not mean that all possible interventions are exclusively at the micro level. But knowledge generated at the micro level must find ways to move upstream to inform some interventions at higher hierarchical levels.

Where there is a risk of polarisation, particular efforts should be made to engage in genuine, meaningful and not just tokenistic consultation with local communities and residents' organisations during 'normal' planning processes. Conversely, these groups should proactively seek engagement in such processes and should be provided with the training and skills, in some cases also the resources, required to fully participate.

Urban renewal is not only a physical process but also a process that triggers social dynamics like envy and a sense of encroachment that come with the new contacts and new visibility of different communities. The externally imposed juxtaposition of different communities, for example as a result of urban renewal processes, seems to have the potential to trigger related grievances.

We found no ultimate proof of the isolation hypothesis, according to which a lack of exposure to 'otherness' leads automatically to polarisation, stereotypisation and in some cases even to radicalisation. We came across some evidence and practitioners' opinions against it but mainly in support of it. Regardless of the correctness of the isolation hypothesis as a universal explanatory model our research shows that what matters at least as much as the quantitative degree of segregation is its spatial level (macro, meso, micro) and its concrete practice in everyday lives. Segregated neighbourhoods might be a completely different thing than segregated storeys within one building. Such issues deserve much closer scrutiny in future studies. The different segregation/mixing levels translate into different types of spatial practices, for different kinds of activities, at different times of the day and year. All of that is not yet understood well enough despite its social and political significance. When implementing policy on the basis of the isolation hypothesis, therefore, we should always treat it with a critical spirit, paying attention to the contextual, socio-material mechanisms of radicalisation, and not relying on the potential 'social fix' of social mix as the universal panacea.

Relatedly, some of the cruder socio-fugal[1] CPTED interventions that are often material elements of gated housing blocks, public spaces and institutional buildings, can signal distrust and work as self-fulfilling prophecies, as well as stimulate stigmatisation and defeatism (see the interview with Frank Gaffikin in Chapter 9). Sometimes, however, they are simply indispensable to save lives, when these are evidently at risk. In this case, the immediate construction of such features is justified. Whether creative versions of such artefacts (like using leafy plants as an anti-graffiti feature, see Chapter 6) can decrease this effect remains unclear. Another and related problem of many CPTED interventions is the obduracy of security artefacts (such as fences, walls and gates), that is, the difficulty to remove them in case the situation improves. Human deterrents (such as guards) are obviously much less obdurate; however, they tend to be more visible, 'blend in' less and don't get filtered out as easily as physical artefacts. Their presence can therefore appear even more conspicuous and difficult to normalise than fixed CPTED interventions. It is therefore unclear whether these agents are a preferable and/or realistic alternative to permanent artefacts.

Drugs (especially alcohol) and a lack of political leadership can increase the likeliness of spontaneous, opportunistic offences. This class of offences is easier to influence through CPTED than premeditated acts of aggression. The absence of drugs might – to a very limited degree – reduce the frequency of opportunistic offences. The management of the Stewartstown Road Regeneration Project, for example (see Chapter 4), is concerned about the availability of alcohol from a nearby supermarket. In Amsterdam, alcohol bans are in place in certain squares (see Figure 7.6). Alcohol licences should therefore be granted only after thorough assessment of all implications.

If on the one hand the absence of political leadership can increase the likelihood of radicalisation (like in Beirut), on the other hand, the presence of strong bellicose leaders can imply the strengthening of exclusive identities and consequential increase of premeditated aggression, such as in Belfast.

Where restless young males are the cause of grievances it is important to understand the underlying reasons for this. In numerous cases, it seems worthwhile to provide facilities for harmless distraction and productive occupation, especially for disenfranchised youth. These facilities for harmless distraction – such as youth clubs, sport centres or even skater parks like the one in Lichtenberg, Berlin (see Figure 6.25), should become more attractive alternatives than 'hanging out' in public spaces. To use another example from Amsterdam, these allegedly unemployed, ill-mannered, disrespectful and visibly non-native young people (although often Dutch-born) spending their time idly in squares and parks was the most frequently mentioned issue of concern in Amsterdam. It was seen by many as publicly perceived cause of a climate of suspicion, stereotyping and condescendence. Working even further upstream of the causal chain, increasing

---

1   Interventions with the intended effect to deter from undesired behaviours.

the size of flats for immigrant families in Amsterdam – who tend to be larger than Dutch ones – is an official and plausible strategy to counter related problems. The rationale behind this measure is that more private space and privacy at home could mean that teenagers don't feel they 'have to' hang out in public spaces any more.

Similar to the obduracy of infrastructures like walls and fences, deeply ingrained habits of avoiding 'others' are often cemented and reproduced through wider spatial and material circumstances (mobility routes, retail locations, etc.). This effect is particularly pronounced in post-war cities like Belfast and Beirut, where the existing urban environment is the result of previous atrocities. Scott Bollens refers to this phenomenon in our interview (Chapter 9) as the 'power of urbanism'. We consider this effect particularly problematic in the context of children because the built environment always acts as some kind of silent socialiser. It signals what is appropriate and it implies for newcomers, including children, a message of what is normal and appropriate. This of course is a non-verbal message and therefore operates below the radar of conscious cognition. It is therefore extremely difficult to question and hardly accessible to explicit scrutiny, let alone democratic discourse. In that sense, people almost inherit the praxis of, say, stereotyping. And the urban environment is part of the transmitting gene. It is extremely difficult to puncture such routines and to interrupt this material somnambulism. Schools, artists and the media play a very important role in this context.

THE BUILT ENVIRONMENT AS FACILITATOR FOR POSITIVE ENCOUNTERS

Like polarisation, also its opposite – de-polarisation, de-escalation and community cohesion – take place and have a material and spatial dimension. We have seen this, for example, in Belfast's Stewartstown Road Regeneration Project and in the synchronised removal of potentially inflammatory posters and graffitis from walls throughout Beirut or the careful orchestration of neutrality in the privately owned Beirut Mall. The study of such 'good practice' examples, where the built environment has been successfully enrolled in attempts to facilitate encounters between otherwise diverging individuals or groups, was clearly the most satisfying, quite possibly also the most significant, aspect of our project. To us, the creation of such shared spaces between different societal groups appears like a worthwhile effort that urban professionals should engage in. This could be their modest but important contributions to the prevention of polarisation and radicalisation. Below are some related suggestions. They include ideas about neutral and shared spaces which are actually not the same. The former are meant to be devoid of any signs of community affiliation. Anyone wishing to enter is expected to leave their identity outside. As a result, such spaces can be somewhat bland. Yet, they are often the maximum of what is achievable, at least initially. In contrast, everyone is allowed to bring their own identity into a shared space but is equally expected not to take offence if others do the same.

Although we have not been able to prove that isolation and segregation directly lead to radicalisation and/or polarisation, the pursuit of neutral/shared spaces still seems extremely worthwhile. We feel confident about this recommendation because we also have not come across any evidence to suggest that creating politically or religiously neutral or shared spaces has negative effects as long as people still have the alternative to remain withdrawn if they so wish. Forcing people to share space is bound to trigger massive opposition and subversion. The involvement of the communities in question is therefore highly advisable in related efforts. Based on our evidence, however, we have to conclude that attempts to 'lure' people to top-down created shared or neutral spaces (like Beirut's Solidere) do not always necessarily fail – notwithstanding their ethical difficulty. For example, in Beirut, the 'neutral' space of Solidere was successively appropriated by the public, when demonstrators filled its squares in the events of 2005 and 2006.

Successful neutral/shared spaces are characterised by some necessary conditions: perceived safety, equal treatment and the absence of potentially offending symbolism. In Chapter 4 we explained how a certain degree of target hardening was necessary for Belfast's Stewartstown Road Project to work, together with identically sized and shaped offices and the dual access design. Beyond such minimal design requirements, the appropriation of neutral/shared spaces seems to depend more on the quality of the design process than on the design content.

This might make it difficult to acquire wholesale support for the creation and appropriation of such spaces. Undue push towards shared spaces is likely to alienate and potentially even further radicalise certain sections of the population (see also interview with Scott Bollens, Chapter 9). A different but related problem emerges if the use of commercially built shared spaces is financially prohibitive for many people, for example because of an expensive high-end range of products. Normative arguments such as multiculturality, democracy, diversity and cosmopolitanism carry little weight in this context. Instead, pragmatic, economic, safety and convenience arguments are of predominant relevance in order to make the use of such shared spaces appealing.

Although pragmatic parameters are paramount, it is still advisable to create an atmosphere of civility and to publicly signal normative expectations in order not to yield the public discourse to simplistic and simplifying tattle. One such way of strengthening collective identity and promoting tolerance can be through art; as seen in Amsterdam (Chapter 7).

What we also found in Amsterdam and elsewhere are attempts to create concrete platforms for friendly encounters and dialogue – for example cafés with programmes of municipal initiatives or other 'public talk' events. Even a bit of self-irony might help to diffuse seriousness and to lighten the mood. An arch near the Leidseplein in Amsterdam proudly features the Latin inscription 'Homo Sapiens Non Urinat In Ventum' (see http://tinyurl.com/cr779zh). 'The fact that such a ribald piece of humour (albeit camouflaged as a pseudo-classical spoof) should be set in stone for generations to come is a fine example of … a culture which openly espouses tolerance in all its forms' (Warburton 1998).

Participation of future users might slow down the process of creating neutral/shared spaces. However, their genuine involvement appears highly recommendable as a means to acquire the necessary knowledge about the local context, people's preferences, fears and concerns about planned new or restructured places and to ensure everyone's buy-in. We are aware that different cities have different cultures of and experience with participatory planning and design and some forms of urban governance tend to embrace it more than others. Some claim that enlightened and benevolent leaders can possess or acquire fine-grained enough information about their populace's life-world in order to provide infrastructures, places and urban artefacts that 'match' it. We are sceptical, however, whether benign leadership can ever successfully substitute genuine participation.

The long-term effect of successfully shared spaces is difficult to predict. They might foster the seeds of mutual understanding, corroborate the already converted or make no difference at all. Shared spaces do not generate automatic benefit, but they do generate new chances and options. These are best harnessed through professional social work and a 'culture' of sharing, which includes events, initiatives, competitions, festivals and the careful transfer of responsibility to the local communities.

The provider of neutral/shared spaces is likely to influence the features and functioning of these spaces. State-provided shared spaces depend on the acceptance, strength and neutrality governance of the state itself. Shared spaces created by private and commercial developers are often universally accepted in sectarian terms due to the alleged colour-blindness of the market. However, these places have a tendency to only attract the better-off and to exclude groups on the lower end of the income spectrum. In our view, shared spaces which are initiated, implemented and managed by grassroots initiatives have the best potential for sustainable change, but their development and impact is often protracted.

BRIDGING GAPS

Interventions in the urban environment are by no means a magic wand to solve the problem of societal polarisation and radicalisation, or a quick fix recipe for social cohesion. Nevertheless, we strongly believe that they can condition what policy-makers refer to as 'breeding grounds' of polarisation and potential radicalisation and thereby accentuate as well as alleviate these dynamics. When we started the project, a built environment-focused perspective on issues that are traditionally dealt with by political and sociological studies was welcomed as something new, or at least with positive curiosity, in academic and extra-academic environments which are characterised by considerable communication gaps between the understanding of political phenomena like radicalisation and built environment studies (see the interview with Jon Calame, Chapter 9). We do not claim to have bridged this gap, or even less to have found the magic formula to make policy-makers and built environment professionals work together in full mutual understanding. We did, however, try our best to facilitate more awareness across disciplinary and departmental boundaries. This book is part of this effort.

9

Interviews

INTRODUCTION

During the design phase of our underlying research project hard choices had to be made. We would have liked to investigate a large number of diverse cities but for practical and financial reasons we had to focus on just a few. We also would have liked to study the chosen four cities from different conceptual angles because our pragmatist outlook makes us realise that among different disciplinary approaches there is never just a single correct one with the rest inevitably being wrong. Rather, we believe that different theoretical angles allow you to see different but often equally interesting things. We were also aware that an even more proactive involvement of practitioners and much longer, more in-depth fieldwork would have added another layer of value.

And while we are still convinced that we found a rather good balance of all these factors we thought that we could nevertheless achieve some of this added value by picking the brains of some of the most eminent scholars in this field through transcripts of interviews with them. These interviews were not conducted during our formal fieldwork phase but deliberately after the data gathering, analysis and first round of dissemination had been completed. This allowed us to prompt conversations with them not just about working hypotheses, speculations and very case-specific issues but about our conclusions, big picture issues and wider lessons for scholarship and praxis.

Frank Gaffikin allowed us to benefit from his long-standing and very detailed insight into the situation in Northern Ireland. He sees himself very much as an 'engaged' academic, who works with communities in the 'swampy lowlands' (Schön 1987: 1) on very concrete issues and therefore has an extremely robust 'grounding' with the everyday reality of divided cities. In addition, he could contrast our findings with the experience he gained in a range of other regions including Chicago and Cyprus.

The US-based planning scholar Scott Bollens has conducted hundreds of interviews with a wide range of people in Sarajevo, Johannesburg, Belfast, Nicosia, the Basque country, Mostar, Barcelona, Jerusalem and Beirut. He is therefore in a unique position to compare our findings with the situation in these other places. He has also followed some of these cities for many years and could therefore contribute a longer-term perspective on many issues.

Jon Calame is a founding partner of Minerva Partners, an organisation which helps to harness the ways in which the traditional built environment can contribute to community strengthening. We wanted to include an interview with him because of his strong hands-on experience as consultant trying to improve the situation in a number of cities, including Belfast, Beirut, Jerusalem, Mostar and Nicosia. His disciplinary background is in art history and historic preservation; another reason why we thought he could complement our interpretations.

Wendy Pullan's expertise overlaps with some of our own case-study cities (Belfast, Berlin, Beirut) and with those studied by Frank, Scott and Jon (Jerusalem, Mostar, Nicosia). In addition her work in – or with partners from – Brussels, Tripoli, Kirkuk, Vukovar, Ceuta and Guben/Gubin extends the range of cases and contexts even further and allowed us to contrast the relevance of our findings even more widely. Also Wendy's background as architect helped us to gain more clarity on certain issues.

We had already been in touch with all four interviewees for some time in one way or another. Jon, his co-author Esther Charlesworth,[1] Ralf and Sara exchanged some emails after the publication of their seminal book *Divided Cities* (Calame and Charlesworth 2009). Wendy and Frank were on the advisory panel of our project; the latter was also Ralf's colleague during his time at Queen's University Belfast. And Scott contributed to a conference session Ralf organised in 2006 on materiality in contested cities. This does not mean that the selection of our interviewees is a result of incestuous convenience. We became acquainted with each other because we worked in similar areas – not the other way round. Likewise, we did not simply devise easy and friendly questions. Rather, we wanted to explore issues that emerged directly from our findings, including unanswered questions, which, we realise, were really hard, if not unanswerable.

INTERVIEW WITH SCOTT BOLLENS

Scott Bollens is Professor of Urban Planning at the University of California, Irvine, where he holds the Warmington Chair in Peace and International Cooperation. He studies the role of urbanism in cities and countries challenged by nationalistic ethnic conflict. He is author of the books *City and Soul in Divided Societies* (2012), *Cities, Nationalism, and Democratization* (2007), *On Narrow Ground* (2000) and *Urban Peace-Building in Divided Societies* (1999).

R.B.:   We clearly share an interest in the role of urban policy and planning in conflict situations at a citywide and neighbourhood level. But what are your views on

---

1   Esther also followed Ralf's invitation to a guest lecture at the Manchester Architecture Research Centre.

the role of micro-scale features like architecture, ornamentation, street furniture, even sometimes interior design for the lived reality of social tensions?

S.B.:   Yes, this is very important indeed. I, like most people, feel and experience the city at the micro-scale; whether it's a neighbourhood, on their way to work, when they go to shops etc. they always experience the city at the micro-scale and that's why it is so important. The meso-scale, or city-scale, is certainly also important for a vision of economic development, job activities and fairness. But what matters even more I think is how people interact with the physical city and that is more at the micro-scale. So issues like ethnic interfaces are extremely important micro-scale issues. Also, how a government tries to manage the evolution of an ethnic geography becomes extremely important to stability and potentially co-existence and this management frequently must address micro-scale dynamics. And of course on the flip side at the micro-scale: If it is partitioned with barriers you are doing just the opposite, you are creating a micro-scale architecture of domination and subjugation.

R.B.:   The built environment always acts as some kind of 'silent socialiser'. It implies and signals what is 'normal', it speaks to or educates newcomers, including children, about the standard way of acting and interacting. It does so without words and therefore reaches the subconscious and is hardly accessible to cognitive scrutiny and democratic discourse. I sense that people inherit the practice of division in a way which might be called 'material somnambulism' – after Langdon Winner. Does this ring a bell?

S.B.:   Yes it does. I think it's the great power of urbanism that it creates things on the ground that then become normal, no matter how abnormal or imposed they are, all of a sudden, as the years go by, it becomes normal and becomes part of the normal landscape. For a child in particular, who is growing up in such an environment, this environment is always already there and the child will accept that this is the way things work. There's nothing distorted or abnormal about it. There's no reason to question what is presented as normal and this can of course reinforce divisions. Now you see the *power of urbanism* – and this is a slightly different issue but closely related to this – can be seen in Israel for example. It creates such facts on the ground and this seems perfectly normal in a way. It creates neighbourhoods and settlements and they're just responding to natural urban growth, it's this seemingly mundane and natural event, this creation of the urban landscape, and it doesn't have – at least not overtly – much to do at all with the conflict. It could be seen as just an attempt to create jobs and housing. But this brings us back to the 'silent socialiser'. Surely such interventions are imposed and they will trigger opposition at first by a range of groups and so forth, but once it's there and after a number of years have gone by, what was initially a very partisan political artefact becomes more normal over time. And this is important for whoever teaches the next generation of young people. When those kids will have grown up and that's just their normal environment, we need to wake them up, so to speak, and to make them understand the historical contingency of their world. So I think the power of urbanism is this ability to act like a natural process, that's not part of the great political debate. And this gives urbanism a lot of power even in nationalistic conflicts because it is seen as something not directly linked to politics and that is exactly what gives it great power; you could almost call this semi-independence. As soon as I'm using the word urban*ism* – rather than planners or plan*ees* – I'm not talking about individuals and great powers, I'm talking about the act itself, the creation of physical facts on the ground. You could almost say the power of urbanism comes from its seeming irrelevance; at least seemingly irrelevance at first sight for the untrained or external observer.

R.B.:   Would you say that this power of urbanism can also be used as a positive force?

S.B.:   Yes, you could use urbanism's power to act for positive change. Just one example which we've seen in Belfast: The creation of a commercial district. And there the vocabulary is all about economic revitalisation, job creation and other issues that are not directly related to the big political, nationalistic issues. But in actuality, the commercial district does have the potential, over a long time, to act as shared space and maybe even to facilitate small steps towards reconciliation and maybe even shared spaces.

R.B.:   The UK government has a particular strategy called PREVENT to tackle various forms of violent extremism. In this context it seems that some expect advice from scholars like us about how the built environment can be enrolled in efforts to counter homegrown radicalisation among Islamist fundamentalists. Do you think this is a naïve technocratic idea or a clever holistic view of understanding the issue? Should built environment studies engage with this issue at all and what is the discourse on such issues in the US?

S.B.:   Well, I've read some of the British responses to the riots in 2001 in Bradford and other cities, the Cantle Report (Cantle 2001) and others talking about the 'parallel lives' of different ethnic groups. I don't think, however, I have sensed a strong expectation as you mention in the context of Islamist fundamentalism – certainly not in the US. Here, I would say that, well, retreatist is too strong a word, but built environment studies are typically involved in crime reduction a lot, but I don't think it is taking on questions of Islamist radicalisation or the question of 'parallel lives', segregation and how to bring people together and to increase tolerance and so forth. I don't see that specific language in American policy documents but really more on the British side where there's more discussion about the relationship between the built environment and how people act, internalise, understand (or not) each other and so forth. It's kind of interesting that you don't see that much in the US. Over here, there's a discussion about how to change public or social housing into mixed income estates and districts. Also about the way to mix races and mix incomes and to give people that used to be concentrated in social housing more opportunities in other neighbourhoods. There is a good study looking at that, but that's I think about as close as we get in the US unless I'm forgetting something that relates built environment studies to race and ethnic issues. It's mostly about crime reduction but not about ethnic and racial mixing, interaction and so forth.

R.B.:   I recently read about a street in Detroit which separates in a really stark way a poor black minority neighbourhood and a quite affluent white neighbourhood – and the situation didn't sound that much different from, say, Belfast.

S.B.:   Well, Detroit is an extreme example. I very much think this is the exception to the American rule. But also if you think of something every US American knows about: We are approaching the 20th anniversary of the Los Angeles riots and so far the discussion has been very limited in terms of the relation between the built environment and race, ethnicity and so forth.

R.B.:   Do you think there should be more attention to these issues?

S.B.:   Yes, I do, and this brings me back to your question whether built environment studies should engage with these issues at all. Although it might mean to slightly broaden the label of built environment studies but yes we should look at issues of integration and dispersal of high concentrated Black African-American and Latino communities from a built environment perspective. I certainly think you need to talk about the relationship between, in particular, residential location and urban inequality of opportunity in the United States. There is still a lot of segregation, a lot of concentrated African-American neighbourhoods, and there are locational obstacles that continue to prevent Blacks and Latinos from having any semblance of equality of opportunity. That discussion should be conducted in the States but due to the attack on anything governmental from the political right, that debate is in the closet now and it is very hard to advance that.

And in terms of the really intensely polarised cities a great policy might be first and foremost 'just doing no harm'. What I mean by that is just trying to prevent putting up those artefacts of partition and division that are hardening the interfaces. In the spirit of flexibility and porosity, try to avoid that as much as possible. During intensive conflict periods partitions could be temporary and this very difficult process of de-walling – which is obviously very pertinent to Belfast – should always be considered. This relates to the criticism that we are trying to engage in social engineering: One of the ways to counter that argument is that we're not necessarily trying to restructure all of an urban area but we're trying to not do harm; we're trying not to create those artefacts of division, to allow some normalcy of urban process later on and to keep your options open.

R.B.:   Social engineering is a good buzzword because some people have accused us of advocating social engineering as an attempt to trick people into the desired way of behaving through the creation of neutral or shared spaces. Would you say there is actually a role in certain circumstances for an almost blunt form of social engineering?

S.B.:   It's the great criticism of what we do and I've heard it a lot in responses to my presentations. And although I'm very careful with my words, I talk a lot about flexibility and porosity for example, but all that people often hear is social engineering: 'You're trying to force us to live together when we don't want to!' It's almost like a reflex that people have when they talk about trying to look at different options for an urban environment. And I can say over and over again it's not housing integration, it's about leaving open the opportunities for people if and when they choose to live together. You know, governments intervene in the urban environment all the time. Governments are constantly engaged in social engineering and in a lot of polarised cities they do it either directly or by sponsoring artefacts of division and partition; not just walls but any sort of activities that indirectly divide or partition neighbourhoods. In the United States, for example, and certainly in other countries too, all these urban renewal programmes and urban freeways are placed in ways to divide and partition different groups. All of that is social engineering. So it's the label thrown out to squash people that are trying to look at their urban environment in a little more sophisticated way, that try to encourage some co-existent viability and not just fall into the ethnic and partisan traps.

R.B.:   Weapons are clearly participants in armed conflicts. Words, especially of the inflammatory type, can also play an obvious role. But we would argue that buildings, street layouts and other physical features can play a similarly important role, yet they fall somehow more easily below the cognitive radar and don't catch the same attention of the media, sometimes also of politicians, maybe because they are in a way quite mundane and ordinary. Would you agree? Is this a problem and if so how can we address this?

S.B.:   Yes, there is a problem and it is related to what I mentioned before, the power of urbanism in that it falls below the cognitive radar. That's the issue with a politicised environment that once built it becomes somehow objective, normal and a fact of life. Protests happen against it at the front end – for example, protests against Israeli development patterns – but once those protests fail and the environment is restructured, the neighbourhood is built, then they take on this normal quality and it can severely distort and predetermine any sort of political debate. These seemingly mundane settlement patterns and acts of building materialise the power of urbanism.

Just to give you an example: The central city of Beirut has been redeveloped in a way that, arguably, has been dominated by free market principles. It is an attempt to create a mundane, more normal and market based central business district. Having said that, it has the strong colour of Sunni Muslim money, and some say that it has been re-established and re-taken back by Sunni Muslims. And there's some reality to that; certainly the leader who sponsored that city centre redevelopment was a very popular Sunni Muslim leader. If you look at the built fabric as a result of a pretty much colour-blind, free market effort, it still has for some groups the stench of a 'Sunni Muslim plot'. So there's a counter-argument that a colour-blind effort is in no way as mundane and ordinary but seen as an imposed decision by one of the groups. In general, I would agree that usually the built environment is seen as mundane and ordinary – and therein lies the power of urbanism. Beirut, however, shows that colour-blind to one group may not be to another.

R.B.:   In your book City and Soul *you refer to a study that shows that those who live in neighbourhoods which are predominantly of the same race, tend to be more hostile in their attitudes towards other groups. This seems to contradict Robert Putnam's findings (2007). He argues that when people are exposed to diversity and realise the confusing plurality around them they tend to hunker down like a turtle. Both positions could have strong planning implications around the question: 'Should we facilitate encounters or not?'*

S.B.:   The findings about the positive psychological effects of mixed neighbourhoods can be found in Eric Oliver's book (Oliver 2010) – and I trust his findings are solid. One guess, and it really amounts to a guess, why Oliver and

Putnam find differences is that Oliver was looking at, for the most part, established neighbourhoods where people of different backgrounds have been living for a while. Whereas Putnam is probably talking more about a short run effect. So this could be a temporal difference between the two. I would certainly think that in the short term, waking up in a mixed neighbourhood would be pretty scary for most people. But diversity might be something that requires some getting used to. And even if you hunker down each day, over time you might discover that there's no real threat there. Everybody seems to be doing their stuff and engaged in all sorts of normal things. Given time, the positive effects Oliver talks about might materialise.

The implications for planning are difficult because if we increase flexibility and porosity – to use my words here – and encourage people who don't mind to integrate then in the short term there could be some difficulties. You know, 20 steps forward and 10 steps back. There could be some volatility and, depending on politics, there could be some regression. But the long term I would say is pretty positive. It's one of those cases where we're trying to just keep a steady oar in the water and it's over a medium term, four, five or six years, that things normalise, given political progress.

R.B.: Something interesting seems to be going on with iconic projects like the Guggenheim museum in Bilbao. It seems to have had a rather positive effect on the social tensions in the Basque country. To what degree is such an approach replicable elsewhere?

S.B.:   I think the lesson from the Guggenheim isn't that you just stick a building there like a magic wand. With that approach people would run into all sorts of big problems. In Bilbao it was not just a building but this whole social process and the wider public discussion about the proper direction for Bilbao. Bilbao was an obsolete industrial city looking for a way to move ahead. It was a dying city, independent of the polarised Basque question. So there's been a long discussion about moving in the direction of arts, to join the international circuit and so forth. A lot of people thought this is absolutely nuts. But there was also some good luck: The Guggenheim Museum was looking for a site and a few of their initial sites did not work out. But it doesn't only come down to luck. It was the overall process. And then the building became very successful in terms of attendance and reinforced that Bilbao could actually pull this off and play a role in the international arts and culture scene. It's not just the building. Planning had a great role in this because the planners put together a central city plan for this obsolete city and in their original plan they actually thought things through and had a site identified as an arts and cultural centre – they had no idea it was going to be the Guggenheim and Gehry and all that. They got it right, they got lucky too but there was also a longer social process. Sticking that Gehry building onto Sarajevo would not come with that process and discussion. It would still be pretty, but it would be at best irrelevant and at worst would be a setback for the city for creating something which is absolutely not in line with its wider context.

R.B.: In a number of cases we noticed the particular role of women for de-polarisation and reconciliation processes. Have you come across similar gender patterns?

S.B.:   I wish I could say I did. Maybe there was some kind of interview bias or I didn't pick up on some issues but among all the nine cities I studied I haven't seen much about women's civil rights issues, women's movements, etc. – apart from Belfast and Johannesburg of course. In South Africa women certainly play a very strong role by not letting the men dominate the conversation – they had a strong advocacy role, by going out and shouting out for the common sense. And there's of course the energy of the women's movement in Belfast. But I did not find this to the same extent in the other seven cities. I hesitate to draw conclusions from this. It might just be the way I was interviewing. But certainly women's movements are very important in terms of promoting peace.

R.B.:   In your book (Bollens 2012) you argue that 'the real barriers to peace are not the physical divisions of the city but are in people's hearts and minds' (p. 66). You also quote Anwar Nusseibeh with a similar statement: 'What effect can the mere shape of a wall, the curve of a street, lights and plants, have in weakening the grip of power?' (p. 233). Conversely, you state that 'focusing on the physical nature of urban space is important because how the urban environment is constructed and organized can be cause, object, and limiter of urban violence, and also establish a range of possibilities' (p. 234). Isn't there a bit of an inconsistency?

S.B.:   That's a very important question and I think there's one particular paragraph in my book (Bollens 2012: second paragraph on p. 235) in which I deal with this. The answer is certainly one of those type of answers where you basically need both, the political advancement or the key to people's heads but you also need to engage alongside in terms of the physical environment. Both are important. You know, without political change or without change in people's minds you can change the physical environment as much as you want; it's not going to make any big influence. But I wouldn't go as far as Nusseibeh in his quote. I think he is making too extreme a statement because as political progress is made, the mere shape of a wall curve along the street, like plans, can make a big difference.

R.B.:   What continues to puzzle you? What questions are unanswered?

S.B.:   What I would love to do – and this links to the issue of process versus content you are working on – is this: You know I studied Jerusalem and Belfast and Johannesburg in 1994, 1995 and it's now almost 20 years later. What I'm very interested in is the dynamics of change and evolution, not only in terms of political dynamics but also urban dynamics over that 20-year period. One could track the changes in the political environment through that period and then look at what has happened in the urban environment. Is it either in sync with that political progress or is it at odds with it? How much does the evolution of urban change lag behind the political progress? It's essentially a timing issue. You know, I was amazed when I visited Belfast again last year, about 17 years after my initial research there. It's fascinating how little has changed in the working-class neighbourhoods but also how much has changed in other parts of Belfast. There is so much talk now about public sector entrepreneurship, the market, new ideas about the city and so on but I would really like to talk about those things we discussed 17 years ago. I am curious whether these dynamics and processes are rounding up or rounding down the conflict.

R.B.:   There seems to be a lack of communication between built environment disciplines (architecture and planning mainly) and studies of conflict (political sciences, international relations, anthropology). Would you agree and how is this being addressed? How, then, is your work perceived by scholars and practitioners in such fields?

S.B.:   Yes, the lack of communication is a major problem – actually on two levels, among academics and among practitioners. If you take urban planning and political science, the Venn diagrams of these two academic disciplines – but also of urban studies and international relations – show very little overlap in terms of scholarship. That's a problem. But also on the ground you see that big gap. The reconstruction of Bosnia, the question of how to deal with displacees in Sarajevo and Mostar, there is a massive lack of communication between architects on the one hand, the built environment, and on the other hand the real political experts from the international community who can talk about power sharing, elections monitoring, etc. But these are like two different universes and that's a problem on the ground.

R.B.:   This links directly to another question: From your findings do you derive certain conclusions for the education of planners and architects; both at the level of university education (BA, MA, PhD) and professional training?

S.B.:   Yes, definitely. This goes without saying. You know, I'm a planner, I'm an urbanist, so I have that frame of mind where I'm always thinking of recommendations and policy implications. My book *City and Soul*, for example, contains very concrete policy recommendations. That's just what I do and that's also what I try to do in my teaching; not only my teaching about these polarised cities but also in courses related to American cities because I see lessons that flow from one type of city to the other. In all contexts we have to try to create an urban environment that facilitates co-existent viability or pluralism that is softer, rather than harder. It's also about better relations, at least in this country, between race and ethnicity groups. And as you know, it's a difficult challenge to make that connection between the physical and the social/political – it's a great challenge.

R.B.:   Which of your publications do you consider most pertinent for readers with an interest in such issues?

S.B.:   For readers who are interested in the nuts and bolts and practical recommendations probably the most suitable publication is my article in *Progress in Planning* (2006). At the human level it's clearly my most recent book *City and Soul* (2012).

R.B.:   Many thanks for this interview.

INTERVIEW WITH WENDY PULLAN

Dr Wendy Pullan is Director of the Martin Centre for Architectural and Urban Studies and Senior Lecturer in Architecture at the University of Cambridge. She is Principal Investigator for 'Conflict in Cities and the Contested State' (www.conflictincities. org), an international and multidisciplinary research project based in the UK and funded by the ESRC's Large Grants Programme. She received the Royal Institute of British Architects' inaugural President's Award for University Led Research for work on Conflict in Cities. Dr Pullan has published widely on Mediterranean and Middle Eastern architecture and cities, especially Jerusalem, and has advised on issues to do with urban uncertainty and security. She is a Fellow of Clare College, Cambridge.

S.F.:   There is one evident commonality between our book and the Conflict in Cities project. Both focus on the ways the urban environment and conflicts are related. However, our book focuses on the process leading up to conflict, whereas Conflict in Cities focuses on the state of conflict. What are your views on these two perspectives on conflict?

W.P.:   I named the project Conflict in Cities and not 'cities in conflict'. For me, there is a primary difference between conflict in a city, and a city that falls into conflict and then may come out of it. Conflict is part of the urban condition and this is one major hypothesis that I have based my work on. Then there is the question of what happens when the conflict spirals out of control and becomes violent and extreme. There is also the question of what sort of conflicts always exist in cities: some of them can be between two groups of neighbours, they can be very minimal, and that is much closer to what you're talking about: things that have the potential for getting worse, but usually don't.

The other aspect, something I'm writing a book on, is a theoretical take on the nature of conflict. It concerns how, over many centuries, conflict is being manifested inside cities. Most of our urban institutions come out of some sort of conflict. If you look at the judicial system and courts inside cities, they are based on adversarial relationships; but they become a way of developing the conflict in constructive ways, of channelling the conflict. Conflict is also different than war. Most wars (although guerrilla war might be more problematic in this sense) seem to have a beginning and an end: they may flare up again, but there's that sense that they start and stop.

The other thing to highlight about Conflict in Cities is the way we chose our case study cities. Some of it had to do with the practicalities of setting up a project and what we could manage. When we started the project, there had been little work done beyond what I would call 'tick box comparisons' between cities. We felt there was more to it, and so we concentrated on Europe and the Middle East, in order to have some basis of comparison. We specifically wanted to gain what I would call a 'temporal spectrum', so that we could look at different times in the life of 'conflict in cities': cities that were coming out of conflict like Belfast or Berlin; other cities where the conflict seems to continue, like Jerusalem; cities that seem to be falling back into conflict, like Beirut. Kirkuk was very interesting, as we could see certain influences on the city that were causing greater conflict. So the study gave us this temporal spectrum that we could look at simultaneously.

S.F.:   In this variety of stages and types of conflict, what are the non-dramatic expressions of conflict that are part of the everyday life of cities?

W.P.:   At the very official level – which I think still affects people's everyday life – in all of these cities there's different groups bringing people together to talk about the conflict. They are mostly activist groups, but they can also be sponsored by official bodies. There is a Northern Ireland Human Rights Council, in Jerusalem there is a joint Palestinian/Israeli group of bereaved people, who lost close friends or family members in conflict, but decided that the only way to overcome it is to learn to talk to each other. That is certainly still a situation of conflict: they don't come together because they like each other, but it is a type of bereavement counselling. It is debatable whether it is mundane or profound, but it's certainly not violent, and it's a way of trying to go beyond extreme measures, like building walls.

If you want to look at it from an urban point of view, we're doing a lot of work on the nature of shared space. Being in a space affects us profoundly: a lot of it is almost subconscious. There's a latent sense of being in the space, a latent memory that builds up over time, and that's very important. You can have different groups who don't like each other, and yet at the same time they may use that space. There is a level of sharing, which is not to say that they like each other, but they may have a certain fairly civilised interaction. Or, they may not have any interaction at all, in using a town square, for example. But even if you take a so-called 'normal' city, like London, there are very few people that we talk to or interact with when we go out into the city. So I think it's important that we don't expect things from these very divided cities that we would not expect from other much more peaceful ones. This excludes, perhaps, those cities that have an absolute division, like Nicosia, where people did not *ever* go to the other side and have had no reasonable possibility of any interaction.

S.F.:   *What is your idea of 'normal' cities and their differences or commonalities with divided cities?*

Let's start with a place like London. It's a big city, many different groups, certain deprived areas, and then you lay a bad economy on top of that. I don't think it's rocket science to see why people went off the rails [during the riots in August 2011]. Many big cities have similar problems at certain points in time. This is what I mean by conflict being inherent to the urban condition: sometimes it does fly out of hand. Then there is the question of how institutions develop that over time. I don't want to use the word 'management': I think the problem is much deeper than conflict management. It means learning to live with conflict, and channel it in certain ways. One of the historical examples I always like is Siena, which had an extremely bloody history in the Middle Ages with all of its *contrade* [parts, quarters] fighting with each other. Slowly they developed a system of urban government (because it was a city state it was more than just simply urban) and, in a modern sense, it was one of the most 'advanced' places in the world.

S.F.:   *Was that power also projected in architecture?*

W.P.:   Yes, within the municipal piazza. And it was more than power; it actually became a way of learning to organise themselves to get along with each other. It wasn't by trying to get rid of the conflict: they actually brought the conflict into the centre of the town, in the Palio horse race. One of the things that we try to do today is to get the conflict out of the city, remove it or banish it. We don't want it in the centre of our cities because we want the centre of the cities to look peaceful and lovely, urban and cosmopolitan. But Siena is a very good example: even today there is the Palio which is competitive and can be violent at times. It hasn't been sanitised completely, although it is a major tourist event – and I am not going to say that we should put a horse race in the middle of Jerusalem or Baghdad and that will solve their problems. In Siena that came out of many many years of negotiation, but it is an interesting example.

S.F.:   The Palio is very 'frontier like', but it is right in the centre of the town: could you connect this example to your idea of frontier urbanism?

W.P.:   Yes. The whole city of Siena is made up of frontiers because of the contrade, and instead of trying to stamp them out, and saying 'Oh no, we're all the same and we all get on with each other' they came up with many different urban symbols; each [contrada] has a little logo, colours, and they depict these symbols on the street corners. People advertise their differences and it's very important to them. What contrada you belong to matters to the extent that, even today, when children are born, people will bring a little bit of the earth from the contrada and put it underneath the birthing bed in the hospital.

If we come back to London, you have whole classes of people who do not have jobs, are frustrated, some of them are poorer than others, but there is no identity there, or their identity is only seen in negative terms. That is problematic. I haven't studied London in any great depth, and the jury is still out for really getting to the details of the riots last summer. But it seems to me that the argument of the government that Britain is 'broken' and we have to fix it, is something that does not take into account that differences can be channelled in ways that are more constructive, and that people can identify with where they live and who they associate with.

S.F.:   But would the authorities or the politicians perceive or account for the positive potential of conflict? Would they consider London [as a conflict city]?

W.P.:   No. Conflict is seen almost completely in negative ways.

S.F.:   Which leads to the question of relevance. The space of the city and the way the city is managed can influence the process of conflict and peace. For example, you argue that Jerusalem is too materially divided to allow the peace process to be implemented. The urban environment is actually hindering the political process. Do you think the representatives of 'macro politics', like diplomats and international politicians take enough into consideration the 'micro' geographies, the concrete side of the conflict?

W.P.:   I don't believe they do. Especially in a very high profile case like Jerusalem. All over the world, Jerusalem is reported constantly. It is, arguably, the conflict that people want to see solved more than any other. There is a constant desire for peace negotiations, but that is seen almost completely in political terms. I do not want to diminish the importance of politics, but one of the things that is not taken into account are the urban aspects of the city, and this is where Conflict in Cities does play a role, because we look at everyday life; we do a lot of micro studies, monitoring situations over a long period of time. One of the areas that we look at is Damascus Gate and we have been studying that carefully since 2003, so we feel we can offer something there that a politician who flies in and out very quickly might not ever see. There is also the question of what is good for the urban everyday aspects of the city and what is good for political negotiations and maybe a peace treaty. They are not always the same. I think one of the reasons we get divided cities is that politicians tend to throw up their hands in despair, they simply don't know what else to do, and the populations are really bleeding at that point, people are getting killed and cannot live properly together. When conditions get very bad the obvious solution from a political level is to divide the city. It is something that is brought up a lot with different cities that suffer these extreme levels of conflict. The problem is that once you physically divide a city, it is almost impossible to put it back together. Take Nicosia, where there have not been any killings in the past 35 years since it was divided: that is important and I don't want to criticise it too much. On the other hand, though, you get two rump cities that are completely separated from each other and neither of them really flourishes well – and it is a capital city!

Another area that we've looked at is the medieval cities along the Polish–German border. The one I've studied is Guben/Gubin. For 800 years these cities were one and they really did flourish; they were major industrial areas. Guben/Gubin was the central hat-making city for this area. They were well-to-do but then at the end of the Second World War, they were divided because the border between Poland and Germany was established along the Oder and Neisse rivers. It was one of the nastiest borders in the Cold War. Now, it is almost impossible to put the halves of the cities back together. There are very well intended people trying to figure out what they might do to solve the problem, and they're coming up with certain ideas; but even with the best will in the world, it's really tough. It is taken for granted that there is an international border through all of these cities, but at least it's an open border: Poland joined Schengen,[2] so people can walk back and forth easily.

S.F.:   Institutionally, it's quite difficult to also have a partnership with the other side.

W.P.: Yes. It's very difficult, even for really small things. This comes back to one of your earlier questions about everyday conflicts: how do people negotiate difference? One example is hearing the other's language: if we're talking about cities that are divided and they have one language on one side and one on the other, like Nicosia for example, once the city is divided one side never hears the other language. Again, I'm not talking about any major communication, but you lose contact with a culture if you never hear them speak; you never see people who look different. It results in vilifying the other side, you forget what the other side is. These are fairly small things, and I have been criticised for making too much of them when I've said that it's important for the Israelis to hear Arabic because Hebrew has become such a dominant language in Jerusalem, that Israelis can live their lives without hearing Arabic. Generally people laugh and say: 'well that's not very much' and I agree: compared to the construction of settlements, it's not very much, but in the long term I think it's very important. We need to be looking at these things in the long term and not just in the short, or medium one, and political solutions are mostly for the short term or the medium term.

S.F.:   So cities absorb conflict and conflict has been part of them. And it's very difficult sometimes to revert back to a stage of unity and sharing.

---

2   The Schengen agreement was signed on 14 June 1985 and formed Europe's borderless Schengen area. Poland was admitted in 2007.

W.P.:   Well just to open the borders and [gain] some level of trust, enough to walk to the other side, or to need the other side in some small way … Sometimes you're not that trustful, but you have some reason to go over there.

S.F.:   Yes, perhaps [the other side] ha[s] infrastructure or something.

W.P.:   Yes, exactly, even if it is just a good pub! I'm just thinking of Berlin, a huge city, with many different centres. One of the problems they've had, is that people got used to being just on one side or the other. People who were either not born or who were children when the city was reunified have always used both sides of the city; [they] don't think anything of it, whereas a lot of the older people still don't want to cross.

S.F.:   There is an obvious parallel with Beirut and younger generations.

W.P.:   Beirut is interesting that way. But because Berlin was intentionally reunified and the outward human differences are much more difficult to perceive because there aren't religious, language, national, ethnic differences, one may say: 'well where are the differences?' But it's very interesting how you still can see some differences. People were brought up in different ways and so even for me, as a foreigner, when I go to certain parts of the former East Berlin I can recognise it immediately from the way it's been built, but also the way the people act, dress, and so on. My ear isn't good enough to hear the accents, but people do talk about the German being slightly different on each side.

You don't always have to have a wall or an international border to make a border. At one point I wrote an article on Road One in Jerusalem, which divides the city (Pullan et al. 2007). There's nothing like a major inner-city motorway to create a division; we find them all over the world, and know they are sometimes used intentionally to divide. So it's important not to say that Beirut is now a unified city because it hasn't had an actual border. Look at the way the southern suburbs have developed. A lot of people from the rest of Beirut are afraid to go there; they don't just wander in, and it's clear what belongs to South Beirut and what not; they know exactly where to go and where not.

Now, you can say New York in the 1970s was quite a violent city and there were areas that the middle classes simply didn't go to, like on the east side you never went north of 96th Street. It was clear: you could actually see how different the city was north of 96th Street. Of course today that has changed. That's the other interesting thing. If you take one of our so-called 'normal' cities like New York, the violence subsided, things did change. There's a lot more integration, Harlem changed: it is possible.

S.F.:   And also, it takes time [for things to change]. Lara Deeb's (2011) work is about the developing leisure culture in Beirut's southern suburbs, as a Shia Muslim middle-class way of entertainment that is obviously not based on alcohol or clubs. But people from outside the southern suburbs, especially people who work in international organisations, start looking at it and actually go for it. But it takes time for the other part of the city to understand that. The timing is different.

W.P.:   Yes, and things may change. But it is people from international organisations, who don't carry the mental baggage that Sunni or Christian people would, and so it's much easier for them to go there.

S.F.:   *Have you got in your work any good examples of how cities can let peace in?*

W.P.:   Yes. I don't know if I'd call it peace, but [perhaps] we can we call it less conflict? Things improve, there's more interaction, we see that a lot. When in Jerusalem we interview either Israelis or Palestinians, they nearly always start by telling us 'you know, this city has two halves, we're two sides and one side never has anything to do with the other, we turn our backs on the other side' and they all make that very clear. What our research shows, actually, is that there's quite a lot of interaction between the two sides. It's not always ideal: a lot of it is economically and ethnically based. For example: you have a restaurant in West Jerusalem; the management will be Israeli and the people waiting on the tables and washing the dishes will be Palestinians. But it's not always that way, even in a city like Jerusalem where there's quite a lot of hatred and distrust and so on, there is a certain amount of shared space on a better more equitable level: the Cinematheque in West Jerusalem, Israelis still like to go shopping in the old city because in the markets, the goods are different and it's much more interesting than going to a shopping mall. Not everyone will go, and certainly in the period of the suicide bombings, you never really saw an Israeli there; but now it's a less violent period, there's plenty of Israelis who go to the old city – so exchange is not only one way. Palestinians are forced to use certain institutions in West Jerusalem; that's typical where a conflict is an occupation and is very entrenched. Yet at the same time there is interaction, it's civilised to a fair extent. I don't know if you could say it's completely peaceful but it's normalised as much as it possibly could be under the circumstances. That kind of activity is very integral to how cities operate.

S.F.:   *This interaction is perhaps more institutionalised in Belfast, through the notion of shared space.*

W.P.:   Well, it is because they are actually using it as a strategy for peace and shared space has become almost an official term. It was something that was taken on by the government, very top-down. That's not to say that it isn't happening. One of the examples that I like very much in Belfast is a coach tour company set up by former prisoners from both sides. They could see there is some economic benefit in having coach tours as they're very popular and, at the same time, it allows the guides to let off steam. We've used them a lot, whenever we've done workshops and so on. I've been on several of them and I'm always amazed at how different the leaders are: some of them are very polished, very professional, but every so often you get one who is just angry and he really tells you how horrible he thinks everything is there. I am not a psychologist, but certainly the possibility of just being angry and telling somebody may actually be useful.

S.F.:   *So it's not only properly trained architects or politicians who can make these spatial interventions, but also the grassroots?*

W.P.:   It depends on what you want to call the spatial intervention, but we've found that sometimes, when you get properly designed and sanctioned interventions, they don't work in terms of bringing together different factions in the population. The Solidere city centre reconstruction company in Beirut is a very good example. A lot of the Israeli urban improvement schemes were not really done to bring together people, and I suppose Solidere wasn't either.

S.F.:   *There is a written intention, though.*

W.P.: Well yes, you get rhetoric with it, but ultimately, you always have to ask when you make big architecture: to what extent is the main aim in showing your dominance in that part of the city? And Solidere falls into that category, and there are many parts of Beirut where that's happening. Certainly [it happens] in Jerusalem. The planning process is very-one sided; we get examples of architecture being imposed; so much of it [Israeli architecture] was built in East Jerusalem and the Palestinians just won't touch it. It's wrong to think that the architects can come in and solve the problems. We set up Conflict in Cities with the understanding that we were not going to try to make new plans for any of the cities. There has been too much planning without enough study, research, and real thought, and we felt that too often comprehensive plans are not working terribly well …

S.F.:   *How is the work of Conflict in Cities perceived by scholars and practitioners in the field of urban studies and architecture, or in the field of studies on conflict?*

W.P.: This is a very multidisciplinary, interdisciplinary endeavour and so it's not always the sort of thing that will appeal to people in a particular discipline. There are people who are interested in cities, in conflict, in ethno-national issues, that gravitate towards this project. So if you put all of them together, that's actually quite a large group of people – some are more specifically interested and some less. At an academic level, I like to think that in certain ways we've carved out a niche here, in terms of trying to look at cities more holistically and to compare them, to contextualise them. There was very little of that being done at the time we started Conflict in Cities, and now of course it's become quite a major field. There's a lot of people who are interested, and it's come much more from geography, sociology, politics and anthropology to some extent, while architecture and urbanism has been generally slower to look at these cities. The urbanists and some of the architects have been much more interested in globalisation and less interested in the role that conflict plays, even though it is of course very much there in the whole process of globalisation. When I've talked to groups in architecture schools, I find that students are very interested. Often it's the undergraduate students who are very much in tune with these things.

S.F.:   *How is Conflict in Cities shaping potential future research by postgraduates and undergraduates?*

W.P.: We do get a lot of enquiries for people who want to do PhDs, for example.

As you know we've had a PhD component as part of Conflict in Cities. These people are now starting to submit their dissertations, so they'll go out and spread the word, but now I have a new group who've recently come in. Some of them are working on topics that are closely related to what we do in Conflict in Cities. We have somebody looking at Sarajevo, but there are also related subjects that can benefit from Conflict in Cities. Very interestingly I have a student who's working on Stratford in the shadow of the Olympics. Clearly there's a conflict, clearly there's a division there; it's not international, but there are a lot of areas in which the student benefits from Conflict in Cities research.

There is an area of study developing and I certainly wouldn't want to say this is all because of Conflict in Cities. But I think that we were probably in the right place at the right time and that has certainly made a difference and produced a lot of general interest from academics.

One of the areas that still isn't understood as well as it might be is ethno-national conflict, boundaries, borders, all of that sort of thing. There's a lot of interest in that, but people often miss something that I think is critical: they don't realise that cities are implicated in these studies as much as are states. This is one of the areas where I can contribute, because I know cities much better than I know nations.

A city isn't just a small state: you can't just transfer an understanding from one to the other. When I started working on the notion of frontier urbanism, the idea of borders was taken mostly from a state understanding of borders. I was using previous research that very clearly had shown there was more radicalisation at the edges of states than in the centres. It wasn't terribly clear what the centre was, whether it was the capital city or what; but in any case, the radicalisation [was] at the edges for various reasons. I thought that I might be able to transfer that idea directly to the city. What I found was that … no, not at all: Radicalisation is taking place in the centres of cities, as much as at the edges.

In a lot of instances it's a hard division, or it may be from fighting a war, like in Beirut, where you get the remains of a border through the centre of the city. Cities are very different from states; the dynamic of cities is quite complex and it's very spatial. It is, of course, social, but it's primarily spatial. Divided cities can't only be seen through social groups.

S.F.:   What still puzzles you in your work, what questions remained unanswered and what are your immediate future projects?

W.P.:   Why do people hate each other in this way? I don't think any of us really understands this question. The Balkans is the best example of that puzzle: how is it that you can have people who live together peacefully for generations and then they turn on each other? And why does that happen? Rwanda is another really good example. What happened in Kigali, where people had been used to living with each other? That's the really worrying thing. I feel fairly confident that we shouldn't be dividing cities, because it really doesn't help at all. But then, people do live together and they have normal relations and they're civilised and sometimes friendships form; they're proper urban relations and the spaces accommodate that sort of thing. You can have good markets, for example, where people meet and there's an exchange. Then all of a sudden it all flares up and people start to kill each other. To some extent the change comes from the national politics. When something flares up in a small neighbourhood or a market, very often it's coming from the national centre, in one way or another. I don't blame the government for everything. Sometimes the problem could be political factions and it could also be coming from what's going on next door, in the next country. I guess the part that we all find really frustrating and depressing is that people seem to be so quick to look at other people who are different and say: 'I don't like you because you're different than me'. We don't understand that very well, I don't know if we ever will.

S.F.:   What are your research plans for the near future?

W.P.:   We're just at the beginning of the last year of Conflict in Cities so we're publishing a lot. We have a book called *The Struggle for Jerusalem's Holy Places* coming out in 2013. We also have an edited volume in preparation. There is quite a lot of project work to complete. The intention of the project was always that we would do a lot of work on the cities individually, and then we would develop ways and means of cross-cutting between them, and then come back to comparative work. That's something we're working on now. As for me personally, I shall be working on a book on the nature of urban conflict. It will be a theoretical book, a lot of it based on what has emerged out of our more empirical studies, trying to make sense of why I feel conflict is embedded and always has been embedded. It's provisionally titled *Urban Agonistes*. It is founded on the idea of *agon*, which means 'struggle'; but I understand it as a struggle that is institutionalised, one that is channelled and that can have constructive or positive outcomes. The term itself and the idea comes from Ancient Greece so it's had quite a long time to germinate. I feel that the historical examples are really interesting and important and I think one of the things that we probably haven't done enough of in this field of studies is to link the history to what is happening today. So this book will be primarily to do with the contemporary situation, but it will be looking at certain historical ideas.

S.F.:   *Thank you for this interview.*

INTERVIEW WITH FRANK GAFFIKIN

Frank Gaffikin is Professor at Queen's University Belfast and Director of the Institute of Spatial and Environmental Planning. His teaching and research profile includes areas such as Planning in Contested Space, Spatial Regeneration, Sustainable Urbanism. He was and still is Principle Investigator in a number of research projects focusing on the role of planning for spatial regeneration and community cohesion. His recent book is called *Planning in Divided Cities* (Gaffikin and Morrissey 2011).

R.B.:   *We share an interest in tensions between social groups and the role of the built environment in this context. However, we seem to focus on different sections of the 'escalation spectrum', ranging from civil-war-like conflict (e.g. Belfast) to much less dramatic forms of conflict (e.g. Amsterdam). Is there a systematic difference for the role of the built environment?*

F.G.:   Yes, there is certainly a systematic difference. Let's just think of some of the key conditions that keep reappearing in the literature to explain how some conflicts become violent: One is that a contest is about something that is regarded as indivisible, especially territory. The issue is structured as a mutually exclusive struggle between losing and winning.

Secondly, certain kinds of issues are particularly visceral and evoke more of an emotive response. For example, tensions around linguistic difference, like in Brussels or Montreal, don't seem to be prone to violent context. Nationalism or religion can be much more so.

Thirdly, the absence of a state which is not capable or willing to be a genuine arbitrator and to provide equal security to both sides can give rise to people feeling the need for self-protection and vigilantism, which then can spur more violence.

Fourthly, where people feel that violence has in some way worked in the past, that it has yielded some kind of movement, then they come to believe that violence is an effective instrument for change.

I think these differences do translate into a different role for the built environment. Belfast is, compared to Amsterdam, prone to more of those conditions, and therefore the built environment comes, over historical periods, to reflect that. And over time then there's almost a reproduction of violence through the built environment that people install in memory.

Think about the Cupar Street interface for example (Figure 4.2). What has actually happened in terms of built environment is that on the Catholic side you have the houses built in the back of the wall (Figure 4.3) but on the Protestant side they have built almost another kind of buffer zone there (Figure 4.4). If you could magically take that wall away, the actual shape of the wider built environment has now lost the grid connection and would still be a certain kind of physical separation and that's the way in which the built environment adapts to these kinds of conditions and that gets instilled in people's urban routine as almost 'natural'.

So one of the problems we have in a place like this now is that even outside the obvious interfaces and peace walls, you get a built environment, which is more and more about cul-de-sacs and narrower notions of defensible space and so on. The whole grid has been lost in lots of areas. Even in the inner city there are so many walls and enclosures. I don't think you get that to the same extent in a place like Amsterdam.

R.B.:   The built environment always acts as some kind of 'silent socialiser'; it always implies and signals what is 'normal'. It basically speaks to, educates, inculcates newcomers (including children) about the standard way of acting and interacting. It does so without words, reaches the subconscious and is therefore hardly accessible to cognitive scrutiny so that it might even be fair to say that people inherit the practice of division in some kind of material somnambulism (after Langdon Winner). Sounds reasonable?

F.G.:   Absolutely. I recently went to the town Famagusta in Cyprus which is a very eerie kind of ghost town because of the conflict between Greek and Turkish Cypriots. I was talking to some young people in their late twenties who had literally grown up next to this enclosed city. It reminded me of those dark fairy tales exhorting children 'don't go down to the woods', etc. I asked these young people who live next to this enclosed dark space what was it like to grow up there. And of course they say that after a while it becomes normal. I think that's part of the psychology of how we negotiate space, the normal becomes unnoticeable.

And that's true of good things and bad things. Think about the natural environment around Belfast which is greatly underused. I'm always mystified why do not more people use something like Cavehill? And when you talk to people about it, it's quite obvious that they don't notice it any more. Well, conversely, people also get used to the more dark spaces and they start to treat them as normal; they internalise the given. That's also one of the problems: How do you penetrate that sense of normality to get a critical reflection on space?

This relates to a wider problem for the social scientist: We think it's feasible to have proactive social interventions that can be somehow benign, but we tend to think of those things in more rational terms, that the force of a good argument can trump the argument of force. However, we don't really live in a rational universe. Many of these issues that generate conflict are emotional, they're intuitive senses about what is right and wrong. They're not reducible to a set of logical volitions.

It's the same with space. When you try to talk to people critically about the way certain kinds of built environment or spaces can generate or reinforce conditions of separatism, the difficulty is penetrating that awareness. People don't think in those terms, they just live it and use it and make do with it.

This also applies to professionals. Although it is their job to shape those spaces, many of them are in a similar situation. I mean, why is it that a planning document for Belfast up until very recently looked like for any other place? Well, partly planners felt they had no professional competence for it and no distinctive remit around this agenda. Many think things are basically immutable and the best they can do is to manage conflict rather than challenge it fundamentally. This is sleep walking through an environment without really a critical eye that reappraises.

The one interesting time in Belfast where some effort was made to really move on was the vision planning process in the mid-1990s and coincided slightly, prefigured the actual settlement of the ceasefires that came with it. The key rationale was: We are so used to this built environment and we accept it as 'given', so we need to step aside and start with a blank canvas, look ahead 25 years and try to see if it's possible to generate certain consensual visions about that future – and then work backwards. There was some purposeful way that helped to open up certain dialogues amongst people as a prelude to some of the other political negotiations that were beginning to open up. But if you're honest, people did have difficulty making that imaginative leap into that blank canvas because in their minds was a formal setting that was determined largely by what they saw as an immutable set of relations. You can maybe make those relations somewhat less violent but you weren't going to fundamentally change the nature of the contest and that the city would therefore physically reflect that. So I think it, it was an interesting attempt but it also showed the limitations in getting people to make that imagined.

R.B.: What is your view on the role of micro-scale built environment features (landscaping, architecture, ornamentation, street furniture, interior design) for the 'lived reality' or 'enactment' of social tensions?

F.G.: They're critically important, and they can be very small things indeed like street furniture, public art; even the painting of railings. Take that site in Ardoyne, for example, the location of these horrific circumstances, where parents who took their children to school were practically ambushed each morning (related Figure 4.18). The two involved schools are one kind of state Protestant school and a Catholic school, literally just opposite each other in a narrow street. The railings on the Catholic school are coloured green, in the Protestant school blue. So even schools which are meant to transcend some of the symbols of politics are in engaged in that kind of business. Why do they colour the railings in very patent political colours? Was it thoughtlessness? Did they just subconsciously reproduce that or what? But even simple things like that give signals about whose space it is. So it doesn't have to be the formal murals or the markings in the paving stones or any of those things, it can be a simple thing like that.

I remember in the case of City Hall in Belfast, big arguments emerging in the 1990s that if the politics of the Belfast City Council were to really open up beyond extreme antagonisms then the building itself had to start reflecting that. Some people on the Republican side said the whole place evokes a Unionist premise with the statue of Queen Victoria, statues to the war dead and so on. Well do you take down those things or do you put other things alongside them that reflect the pluralist city? That conversation has been ongoing in the City Hall and they have been making slow steps; including small things like using the public ground around the City Hall for other events that are not legible in terms of the local conflicts; things like the European Food Market and so on. So to experience it in a different way from the traditional association that it has had and to blur the political partisan viewpoints in some ways.

I think in micro-spaces like that, deliberate attempts to rewrite the space can be an important part of recreating a different opportunity. Underlying this thinking is a concept of space as something, which is not static and not a passive stage in which the theatre of social life plays out but is itself an active agent. Also, most spaces don't have intrinsic immutable meanings but gain their meanings through relationships. If we accept that, it becomes clear that if you try to change these relationships then the influence of particular micro-spaces on macro-contests have to be regarded. There are certain spaces that carry such a weight of symbolism and history that, if you were to deliberately use those as opportunities to redefine not the just physical landscape but also its symbolism, then we are close to a new approach to the conflict and this is extremely important.

R.B.:   Some people misunderstand our approach as a call for social engineering; as an attempt to 'trick people into the desired way of behaving'. Would you say there is actually a role for such an approach in certain circumstances? Or more nuanced – as we would have it: Is there a role for enlightened self-facilitation towards whatever has been collectively agreed as desirable social practice?

F.G.:   This argument about social engineering is often untruthful really, because social engineering is going on all the time anyway. So it's not social engineering versus non-social engineering. If you have a conflict that shapes the environment, which, in turn, begins to shape the conflict then you have some kind of social engineering going on all the time. A deeply segregated city is inevitably a form of social engineering because all sorts of things flow from it. Sometimes it is suggested that people who want to do something actively about the conflict are social engineers and that this is some kind of dishonest manipulation of people. My argument would be that if you don't do anything about it what you are in fact doing is letting a passive form of social engineering still work its way through. So I think in practice you do need proactive social engineering. Of course, this is where ethics comes in, and what is important to me is that you are as candid as possible about that agenda and you put it out there for proper critical examination and discussion amongst the relevant stakeholders. That way, your argument of how a particular intervention – engineering attempt if you like – could make a difference in this or that way becomes part of the open candid debate.

This is not a call for what today is increasingly referred to as agonistic debate, where people put out ideas for open discussion and exchange, pretend complete disinterest, stand by passively and expect that through some spontaneous combustion a long-standing conflict and its cognate built environment will change. That's foolish. I'm in favour of social engineering but I'm in favour of it being part of an honest, open discussion.

R.B.:   Some STS authors investigate the obduracy of artefacts in general and cities in particular. In the context of contested cities does this mean it is always easier to build something, especially makeshift artefacts of a defensive and divisive nature, than to unbuild them? If so, this would mean that distrust always trumps trust for amazingly mundane reasons.

F.G.:   I think that's true. Generally speaking, it is easier to build something like a peace wall or some kind of public artefact which reflects a particular partisan view than to take them down. Look at what has happened here in respect to war murals. There's been some progress on changing their character to something more cultural and educational and so on but it has provoked a lot of hostility. It is also something that a number of the community gatekeepers discovered as useful bargaining tool for other kinds of things. So it still remains an instrument of power. That's why the corollary for me is that you need to be very careful before you start building things like peace walls, because while they may offer a temporary solution to something, security and so on, it becomes very difficult to persuade people then to give up what is seen as some kind of new comfort zone.

So what is the reverse implication? What about more positive things that move the situation in a desirable direction? Would they be harder to take down? That gets to the very core issue of trust, which is among the key universal forces of change that fit alongside these particular forces of conflict. For example, if you go to many places I have seen across Europe, there is a proliferation of surveillance and CCTV cameras. And each time they're put up – particularly in deeply conflict situations like ours – you can be seen to have a reasonable cause to do so. Well, the technology is getting cheaper all the time, it becomes easier to install them and now you find them even beyond the typical conflict areas. You cannot go anywhere without these cameras being present. And even in societies less prone to conflict, if you go to the Irish Republic now, again the cameras are all over the place.

I recently stayed in a nice hotel on the outskirts of Dublin; a nice place with a really pleasant lounge, which is a very congenial space for meetings and discussions. I noticed a camera and told the manager: 'Look, I had a lovely stay as usual but could you tell me what is that camera doing in that room?' And of course the answer was: 'Oh well, the camera is not invading privacy and it doesn't pick up any conversation, but, you know, it is there as a protection for the hotel management if somebody makes a claim they've fallen over or something like that. It helps our insurance policy.'

I have talked to a lot of people recently about that issue of cameras. And you get an endless number of justifications. Each one in itself seems harmless but the cumulative effect of it is the notion that as a group of people occupying a space we cannot trust each other any longer, that everything has to be watched. So I think it's a bit like you are saying with the artefacts themselves: When you lose trust it's hard to build it up again. And there is something about a hidden infrastructure of trust, which has to be nurtured and consciously valued. We must not treat it carelessly because – just to stick with the example of surveillance – if we say this is the only way we can all feel comfortable with each other then implicitly you're saying we can't trust each other any longer. And there probably is a tipping point where distrust reinforces the tendency for more and more ramparts and so on.

R.B.:   Some governments seem to expect advice from built environment scholars about how to tackle more effectively the challenge of Islamist radicalisation. Do you consider this a naïve technocratic idea, a clever and holistic view of the issue, something in between or something completely different? Should built environment studies engage with this issue at all?

F.G.:   I think they should in the broad sense because in my view the built environment is all about relationship. This issue about militant Islam or other forms of radicalisation are about relationship in the broader sense. Therefore I think it is reasonable. But there is a real difficulty in the sense of a political process because if you are trying to instrumentalise the built environment in a certain way without it being explicit you have an ethical problem. And if you don't put those issues openly on the table, if you were to operate in some underhand way, that would be counter-productive in many ways.

We actually had an extreme but real case, the controversy in Small Heath, an area in Birmingham, where they detected hidden microphones in trees, etc. Any attempt of this kind is, in the end, counter-productive. Instead, where there is an area with intensive likelihood of a certain kind of problem, why can't we say let's look at the whole range of issues of the public realm in this area, like separate versus integrated schools, housing issues and so on and discuss all the relationships around this kind of built environment. I can't see a reason why that cannot be expressed openly in a transparent dialogue.

R.B.:   Based on our research we concluded that as important as the content of certain design interventions is the process through which this intervention comes about. This is essentially a call for a participatory approach. Would you agree?

F.G.:   Yes, but the problem with that can be that it's like saying you're in favour of apple pie – who can be against that? We have, especially since the 1960s, a whole rhetoric around participation and engagement. This was in many ways a direct reaction to many top-down post-war projects like highway developments, inner-city clearance and so on. People said you've thrown the baby out with the bath water, you've lost community, you've not negotiated with us, etc. This generated a call for more participation. Almost everybody agrees with that but the problem is how to operationalise that. So even if you sincerely try to go beyond a merely tokenistic form of engagement – near the lower rungs of Arnstein's famous ladder of participation – what you typically get when you issue an open invitation for a public meeting is that particular vested interests tend to dominate the discussion; usually developers on the one hand and conservationists on the other. So it's usually a dialogue between those two and the average public give some constraints. And even if you use something more sophisticated or ambitious like *Planning For Real* exercises: Maybe they can make it real for people who are not used to the vernacular of planning and all this, but in my experience they still end up with people who just want to push through their wish list. There is rarely a sincere search for creative solutions and especially about trade-offs. You know, if you want to make any intervention in the built environment, there are inevitably priorities and choices to be made. You can't have everything. There are prices to be paid and opportunity costs. And rarely in these engagements are people challenged like 'if that's what you want, do you realise these consequences, are you prepared to pay that for that and so on?' So in my experience they are more tokenistic, hollow and at worst tick-box exercises to comply with regulatory requirements.

We have it here in an even more formulaic way. We identified some groups for the so-called Equality Agenda, which has to be formally consulted before certain major changes. What happens is that it becomes ritualised. Yes, we need to talk to the disabled, to the elderly, to young people, etc. You ask representatives of these groups a few questions, you come back with some answers but there's no real sense in which these people are really shaping the decision. So I think the real problem is how do you do participation in a truly meaningful way? If you were to be cynical about it you could say: 'Well, in practice most people are simply not civically literate enough to make a meaningful contribution and it's being condescending in the end to pretend that they have that capacity'. Therefore, it might be simply reasonable, and not elitist at all, to say that those people – call them lobbies, experts or whatever – with some training, skills and detailed critical ideas should participate in such forums? From this point of view, the notion of giving people what they want when they don't know what they want – because they've never had an opportunity to be educated about the options – is a complete misunderstanding of democratic planning.

So these are interesting questions because in my experience of over 30 years with a lot of engagement and participation work I would have to be honest and say, as our article (Brand and Gaffikin 2007) covered to some degree, that a lot of it is more tokenistic than real.

R.B.:   In some cases we noticed a particular role of women for various forms of de-polarisation efforts. Have you come across similar patterns?

F.G.:   The role of women is interesting because in many of the exercises I'm talking about, the composition of the audience – particularly the more open audience – there are overwhelmingly women; in our part of the world anyway. And the more local you get when you try to engage people around space in an open public meeting it'll be dominated by women. But when you move beyond that and try to form some kind of ongoing group that will monitor what we want to change, those women tend to suggest men. There seems to be an interesting gender dimension about who has an interest in the built environment and space generally but then who has the right or the best means to shape it? When we get to that part it's still a male-dominated world. And yet, we know that the way in which men and women use skills – particularly so in conflict situations – is very important.

This is very rarely acknowledged as a distinctive part of the way we need to look at pluralism in space.

R.B.:   What are your conclusions for the education of planners and architects?

F.G.:   Much of the old training emphasised a lot the technical skills about zoning, design, software and so on. All of that is important, but it encourages the notion that these issues we are dealing with – which are at their root social issues – have design or technical solutions. I think planning courses, both at the university and vocational level, need to reflect on what kind of education will deliver best the holistic planning they now lay claim to. If you take these claims seriously then what are the skills of people-interaction, of facilitation, of public discussion, of the interdisciplinary dimensions you need to understand what is going on in society? What is also very important, and is very difficult to get students to relate to, is theory. Students often say 'Oh well we have to do some theory, right?' and then the wall comes down. It's just something they painfully go through. To them it is just some kind of abstraction and bears no relevance to the real world. I think there is a rigorous and proper role for theory in planning courses to provide opportunities for real critical examination of what it is we're trying to do here. What is the kind of world we're intervening in? How would you understand this or that phenomenon and so on? This becomes very important and I still think we don't do enough of that.

I also think that learning through action like planning-for-real gives students a more practical hands-on experience in such modules. And this is what we try to do here. But we emphasise to students when we go out to certain communities 'we're going to work with them, but we're not going out as some kind of consultancy'. And to the community we don't just say 'if you let us work in your community and allow these students to get this experience then we'll respond to what you want and we'll help you translate that in planning and design terms'. We go out to these people in the community and say 'we want to do this in a partnership and this means that you have something to say to us, maybe something critical. But we also may want to say critical things to you'. We want this to be a relationship based on honest exchange. We don't come in without values. We as a department, for example, have a certain view about what makes a good place. We may be wrong and we certainly should be subject to challenge in that view but we're not going to pretend we don't have that view. So if someone asked us for help to segregate more, reinforce ghettoisation, etc., well then we're not the people they need to talk to. If, however, they're interested in more connectivity and in a more open city and they want to look at issues of permeability and how that can be facilitated, yeah, we probably are the people they should talk to.

So I think the students in the learning process have to pick up that sort of thing. They have to see that, if they end up working for a consultancy or even for the public sector, if they go into interventions where from the very start they are not explicit about what that relationship is then they're going to be in a difficulty. So I think all of those things are a part of interdisciplinarity, values and ideology, and an emphasis on theory of understanding what is a very complex changeable world. Students should experience first-hand that they should not and must not pretend to be some kind of neutral, technical, apolitical kind of thing. And such issues should be central to planning education.

R.B.:   Which of your publications do you consider most pertinent for readers with an interest in such issues?

F.G.:   Well, the recent one (Gaffikin and Morrissey 2011) was an attempt to bring together a lot of thinking I had been doing for some time. It is structured to some degree to appeal to students. It starts with a more general overview and analysis of what is happening to cities in general to understand the contemporary urban condition as such before it deals with cities in conflict. Division can then be understood in a very differentiated way as well. The situation in divided cities is never of the kind where you can take an easy model from the shelf and prescribe how to fix the problem. Effective interventions require a very thorough understanding of the whole set of very complicated factors. My book is such an attempt to get an overarching view of the issues and to provide some composite reflection of a lot of work I've been doing for a long time.

R.B.:   What are you currently working on?

F.G.:   The main project we're working on at the moment is a half a million grant from the EU PEACE III programme, which looks at a way in which you could construct a model of planning and urban design that would be more applicable in conditions of extreme division and extreme segregation. It starts from what Dumper refers to as the central paradox, that planning in contested situations can inadvertently accentuate the division rather than ameliorate it. Taking that as a question, how can you reverse that and how can you make planning more productively facilitative of addressing these kind of issues? We're looking at it both at a macro-level – the international context for a place like Northern Ireland – but we're also looking at it at a micro-level. So we're taking North Belfast as a micro-geography, where we've done a lot of work with a range of communities. We're trying now to look at the whole area and to see how we can get better links and better connectivities with all sorts of interventions, community-led, public and private. The challenging kind of research question for us is 'what is the spatial unit of analysis that is effective in different circumstances? How local and micro do you go? And how do you link that into meso and macro?' There are all sorts of questions around that and that's mainly what we're looking at at the moment.

R.B.:   What still puzzles you in your work? What questions are unanswered?

F.G.:   I've talked about this to a lot of people of my lineage if you like. When you come to your early sixties, you've been at this for the best part of 40 years, you keep doing the same thing, even though you promise yourself you're not going to do that and you keep wanting to find the holy grail because you're disappointed with some of the things that you have been doing up to now. So what is the elusive thing that you think is still difficult to get in all of this? Well, if you start off – as I do personally – with an ideology of democracy, with a conviction that people get more opportunities to shape the social environment in which they live and if you spend a lot of effort investigating, facilitating and arguing for this but you have to acknowledge that it's not easy to get there and that some of the effects are questionable then you can get quite disappointed. Whereas, conversely, some of the interventions taken in ways that you are ideologically more opposed to or at least have more reservations, such as the free market, can sometimes achieve certain things better, right? [R.B.: For an interesting empirical study on this see (Mele 2012)]. So for ideological reasons I don't want to accept that. But I can see some examples of where that can happen. You can get a situation in a highly politicised partisan situation, where market players come in and say 'we're colour blind in terms of the conflict, we're interested in profit and we're going to change the built environment in this way'. By doing so they can create certain kinds of interventions that, if a more public or political instrument was used, would be opposed by partisans on either side. Whereas people find it more difficult to oppose the invisible hand of the market, which doesn't seem to have a political axe to grind. That's a paradox for me, which is uncomfortable because I think in the end a market driven response will produce other kinds of fractures and inequalities of social segmentation and so on.

So these questions are leading me to spend a lot of time reading philosophy and theology books, more than your typical social science books. Take the contemporary British philosopher John Gray for example, author of the famous book *Straw Dogs*. His basic proposition is that we humans are really just another form of animal and we delude ourselves that we are some kind of distinct species. Even though we accept something of evolutionary theory we still think there's been some kind of wonderful leap to the stage where we're at. And this hubris makes us dream of all sorts of utopias and chase after the illusionary paradise. For Gray, however, utopia is a very dangerous place. And if we look at the attempted utopias, and the twentieth century in particular, they ended up in Stalin's gulags, Hitler's death camps or the killing fields of Pol Pot. And there is a reason for why that happens. It's the tendency to deny the frailties of the human condition and the limitations of what is possible in terms of social change. If we go for this notion of history that we once had some kind of primitive stage paradise that we lost and the effort should be to be paradise regained then we can only fail. The promised land is a futile, dangerous and inherently totalitarian venture. We have to accept that we live in a more frail and fragile world.

So if you conclude from that that the world is not perfectible but improvable then the question is 'what is the level of improvement that you can try and attain at any one time?' And is it better to be more realistic about incremental changes rather than to make giant leaps at any given time? Those are the kind of things that are troubling because it's the nature of human life because we all have a very finite period of active human life we want to see change within those time limits. We don't want to accept that it's possible to conceive a progressive change in a much longer evolutionary period and so we kind of rush to those kind of things which are maybe brick walls. But being realistic again, I don't expect that there is any answer to that [laughs].

R.B.:   *So even if you had a two million grant you couldn't produce empirical data to answer that question?*

F.G.:   I've often thought of that two million grant kind of thing; often by way of the lottery. So if you used that money to bring together a whole set of people that you felt were on the same wavelength and so on and even if you had some kind of critical mass and an intensive period of time trying to unlock such issues – would this work? You know, I have concluded it probably would not.

I worked a lot with people who spent much of their lives in various political forums like the Communist Party, going to endless meetings, always with this hope and agenda that there's some kind of thing going to unlock just round the corner. They have to now reflect critically and say, if they are being honest, that so much of that effort was not only useless but maybe not helpful in all sorts of ways. I mean it is really difficult to confront those of us that in the 1960s could bang a drum on a particular march behind a particular banner, roughly speaking rooted it in some kind of Marxism.

But when you set that aside as a prescriptive answer to problems, it may still be helpful as an analytical understanding of some aspects of the problem – and I think Marxism still is. But when you pull the whole value carpet out under one's feet then the danger of course is that you lapse into a kind of post-modernist relativism, that all sorts of truths are possible and that any notion of some kind of clear universal truth is delusionary. The danger with that approach is – like all cultural relativism – that it loses any anchor, any kind of value system of where you want to go or what you imagined the good society is. So I think that's the problem for a lot of people, like me, my age, my kind of biography. They can no longer feel happy in a home like Marxist theory but there is no easy alternative. And even though they've maybe spent the last few decades trying to eclectically put together a hybrid version that draws on the best of Marxism but some other influence as well, it still ends up very unsatisfactory as a framework, for effective intervention. Well, that's a very depressing conclusion [laughs] but it is, you know, pragmatic.

I would call this principled opportunism if you like. You look for opportunities and try to reflectively make the best of whatever circumstances but they are underpinned by some principles and values. But at the end of the day when I look around me I still see the power of ideology, including theology, to mobilise people with incredible energy and drive and purpose. And those of us who are more critical of various belief systems and more circumspect about ideological truth claims then by definition we don't have that same energy. There is something about being able to rally people to a cause behind some clarity of an ideology that says 'this is the answer'. Whereas if you're no longer in that mould, you lose something of that energy. I don't know the answer to that, but in any given situation where you have two sets of people – some with a clear ideology and others more questioning – you'll find that the ones with the clear ideology are the ones who will maybe drive the situation. In other words, you don't want to get to a stage where your self-critical appraisal of things is so immobilising that it ends in inertia.

R.B.:   Many thanks for this interview.

INTERVIEW WITH JON CALAME

Jon Calame is a founding partner of Minerva Partners. A decade of field-based research on urban partition and post-conflict revitalisation is summarised in a book entitled *Divided Cities: Beirut, Belfast, Jerusalem, Mostar and Nicosia*, published in March 2009 by the University of Pennsylvania Press as part of its 'The City in the 21st Century' series. In 2009–2010 he received the Rome Prize for historic preservation and in 2007 was a senior Fulbright Fellow in Cyprus studying the Nicosia Master Plan team.

S.F.:   What are the processes that lead to urban partition? Is there a professional complicity among urban planners in partition?

J.C.:   The work that Esther Charlesworth and I did (Calame and Charlesworth 2009) was trying to get at this exact question of what the process of partition is. It's so easy and so tempting to get caught up in the surface narratives of urban partition, because it's dramatic, intense, important, a lot of people are suffering – and I wouldn't discount that for a second – this narrative is wildly complex, almost a hopelessly entangled series of social conflicts. But the result of our research suggested that if you dig down there are less esoteric, less complex, more ordinary explanations for how it comes about and a lot of those have to do with the political manipulation of a fragile system. To oversimplify it: you have politicians that at a given moment in time believe it is in their best interests to provoke a dormant conflict between two groups that have had a historic problem with each other (let's say Greek and Turkish Cypriots), and they say: 'we need something out of this situation, it behoves us to create a fight over here to distract attention, to absorb energy, to allow us to come in as a third party mediator'. Obviously the exact motivation is different, but in most of the cases we looked at, one did not have to be a genius to find the political motives that might have driven the initial provocation that sparks the match that goes on to this dry wood pile of real or imagined historic animosities, which then leads to violence.

We need to look back at the primary actors, the people who flipped the switches at the very beginning, before there was any riot or any wall, to see why they might have flipped that switch and what they gained or lost in that process. We didn't go nearly as far as one could or should go, but based on what we learned in each of the five cities, we attempted to sketch out cases where you could say: 'it doesn't take a PhD to see that this or that political group had something to gain'.

And the fact that they had something to gain doesn't mean that they provoked the conflict, but it gives us a reason to look further, and a lot of the literature on this subject doesn't look as much as it should at those core causation factors, those initial levers being flipped. It tends to dwell in the actual material stuff of the partition: how did the partition work, what did it do, how did it cut part A off from part B, what was the impact of that?

I'm very interested in that too, and for regular people that's what matters. Their lives are ruined or compromised by partition or in some cases may be improved. However, no matter how long you spend looking at the impacts of the physical partition itself wondering how it might have been done better or worse, in my opinion – like any kind of disease – until you go back and figure out the cause of the initial infection, no amount of rethinking the symptoms or the downstream affects is going to get you where you want to go. We want to help the next cities that are likely to be partitioned, or that are vulnerable to partition. I really mean vulnerable to being manipulated by politicians to divide and conquer. I'd like to develop a rhetoric of urban partition that allows at risk (urban) communities with a history of ethnic conflict to see some of the warning signs, just as you would see them in yourself if you felt like you were getting sick, and do preventative medicine. That's where our role is as analysts, as people with the luxury of this distance to scan; that's where we could really make a contribution and there's a lot of work to be done.

S.F.:   Is there a difference between divided cities or cities prone to conflict and 'normal' peaceful cities?

J.C.:   My sense is that if we were to try to generalise about how the initial spark turns into an actual fire, then there's a lot of cities in the world that are essentially full of potential conflicts between different ethnic or racial groups, cities that have tension and history of problems and where people don't have a lot of money. Yet most of these cities don't end up with any physical or even legal partition. It takes more than just inter-group conflict, and it takes more than local politicians that might like to see the conflict get worse because they would profit from it. These are all common motives, but they're not enough. They are not sufficient to take us to this extreme, final stage of actual physical partition. So what else is needed for it to go that way? That's one of the questions we were attempting to answer when comparing the five cities. One part of it is that you need a very powerful third party actor, a political actor to – purposefully or accidentally – augment those local politicians' petty power play. There's always local people who would love to do a power play, and would not hesitate to exploit inter-group tension, but what gives them the extra edge? It's usually the presence – direct or indirect – of a larger and more powerful entity, usually an entity that comes from outside the national boundaries of the state that contains that city. In the case of Cyprus, for example, the United States constituted that swing factor. There had been all kinds of minor skirmishes between north and south Cypriots, and people who would have loved to have seen it get worse or get better. However, that was just the kind of low grade tension that was always there. The Cold War then made the United States get extremely interested in having surveillance military outposts in Cyprus, which was physically the closest they could get to looking at Soviet missile bases, then later Saudi, and other air bases. Suddenly that was like the 'X factor': the United States and Britain wanted these sovereign bases because they needed to put their best spy equipment up on Cyprus' mountains. It's all ordinary in a way, but it wasn't to them, it was really important. The United States didn't set out to divide Cyprus so they could have their bases. But there was a moment at which they saw a potential obstacle to their military presence, which was Archbishop Makarios who wanted to get rid of foreign military units, and maybe unify the island. So basically Kissinger made sure that Makarios was taken out, they tried to kill him and he lived, but he was forced out of power. Makarios left a vacuum that let in more venal, low grade politicians in Cyprus. Which is all just a roundabout way of saying that the pile of dry sticks was there and there were occasional little sparks, but they weren't going to set it on fire, until the United States came in and pushed it to the breaking point, and when it started to break, the United States and Britain were only too happy to watch things descend into chaos because the chaos meant that a lot of energy was going to be driven away from them. I don't want to oversimplify it and I'm not saying that there's some conspiracy theory thing behind every single urban partition – there's a lot of responsibility on the shoulders of the local people and I wouldn't want to let them off the hook – but I do think that it requires an X factor, an often external agenda that allows the partition to go forward where it normally would be halted.

S.F.:   In our previous correspondence, you mentioned that the book had very little impact with politicians and diplomats. Why do you think there is a lack of interest towards the urban side of conflict?

J.C.:   I wish I knew the answer. I wonder about this a lot. In our previous correspondence you mentioned the West Bank settlements and Jerusalem. I too thought that would be the issue that would bring more attention to our book, because in order to have a much larger conversation about the internal logic of urban partition, we wrote an epilogue about the ongoing division of Jerusalem. So we thought this would be the reason why policy makers might get interested: because they care about the resolution of the Israeli-Palestinian conflict. That certainly wasn't the case, and I am confused about that, because almost anyone who's informed about the Middle Eastern diplomacy situation will eventually point to Jerusalem and the settlements and the Green Line as key factors. If that is true, then wouldn't you as a policy maker want to know as much as you could know about all the different facets and angles of the problem? One of which would be the analysis from the city partition side, outward to its root causes, which we attempted to sketch out. That didn't happen. Decision-makers live in a world that is so policy-driven, very abstract, large scale, very much about diplomatic interactions, at a very esoteric level. They're so used to ingesting statistical data, they're not used to any kind of data coming in a different form. By studying cities and the behaviour of cities we can actually learn something about the larger dynamic, because these cities are like a microcosm. They're like a stage on which things are enacted, that may have relevance in the much broader arena, and our book is one of many studies that essentially says: 'we think any given city might not matter in the larger scheme of things, but if you study a city properly you might learn something about the thing that's happening next'. I don't think that underlying argument registers with the people who actually make the decisions, like in the US State Department, or the UN. I don't think they're used to taking in data about the built environment, it's like a foreign language.

Likewise, but in reverse, the built environment professionals are inarticulate and almost illiterate in terms of policy. We don't speak the same languages, but the key thing is that they have all the power and we have basically none yet in certain areas we're the ones who know what the key factors are, so we know what to look for. In this case they're missing something important. We're like these tiny little specialists at the mercy of whatever client or boss and they're the ones cruising around the world trying to solve problems or – in my opinion – create them as much as solve them, if I look at the reality of my government's actions.

This brings us to the question of training and curriculum because, not surprisingly at least in the American context, we just keep on talking to each other, it's like preaching to the choir, we don't make any serious effort to extend the meanings and the insights from our domain, over the fences into other domains. We're not even trying to speak these foreign languages, and that's dumb, because we're pretty powerless as a profession, we don't have influence over the issues that have influence over what we care about – cities or the people who live in cities. There are a handful of programmes in the world, all of the ones I can think of are in Europe right now, but there's a handful of programmes that are really trying to bridge these gaps and that's wonderful, but for the most part we don't speak those policy-centred languages and policy makers definitely don't speak ours, so it's a failure of translation. Meanwhile, I don't think the policy makers believe they have anything to learn from insights that are generated at this scale and the kind of concrete level that our work usually involves.

S.F.:   Has this got something to do with the relationship between the university and the city?

J.C.:   Certainly in America there's a total disconnect between the university setting and the real problems as we find them in the city, and also a disconnect between scholarly researchers in the field and the decision-makers. When you're lucky enough to be in the university getting a professional degree, especially as an urban planner, you know that your pay cheque is going to eventually come from a municipal government or clients that may be tied into governments. In other words you know you're going to have to learn to get along with these policy makers. One of the things we're discovering is that policy makers have made some mistakes and, maybe even purposefully, made things awful for people. Then as an urban professional you've got a super-problem on your hands, because you're about to comment in a very unflattering way about the institutions or even possibly individuals that you ultimately might need to pay your pay cheque. That's where the complicity comes in. If you feel like you have to decide between saying what you think is true about the dynamic relationship between politics and the built environment and biting the hand that feeds you, most people are going to be conservative and not bite the hand that feeds them. By doing that, of course, we forfeit the insight that we gain from studying. So there's a built-in conflict and contradiction, especially with respect to urban planners, and in our interviews with urban planners in the five cities, especially in Belfast, people lamented this 'lock-down' situation where they wanted to do the right thing, and yet they didn't because that was their boss they would be criticising. This is a really fundamentally messed up part of the system and most people don't talk about it as far as I can tell.

S.F.:   What has been a good teaming up where the built environment has been tackled or organised or planned in a way that has resulted in more harmony, co-existence or even reconciliation?

J.C.:   The first and easiest one is the Nicosia master plan team. On paper, that is by far the best example of continued collaborative work across the political line of partition to maintain professional relationships. You cannot point to very much success in terms of actual physical projects. The master plan team, which continues to work together to this day over the green line, has lots of lovely plans on paper which is hugely important because if and when there is a settlement in Cyprus, those plans could be activated, saving time and discussion. I give them total credit for having done all this work, but one objectively has to say that they haven't been given much of an opportunity to implement those plans. So, you don't see much from this, but the work that's been going on behind the scenes is lovely and the simple version of that story is a group of individual urban planners in Cyprus who knew each other, worked together and went to school together before the partition, said: 'We are professionals, we are not politicians, we will not allow the political divide to cut us off from each other because we like each other, we respect each other'. In other words, they decided they were not going to allow that beautiful professional ethic and relationship and friendship to be burned up in the general bonfire of the division. It was with personal integrity and individual relationships that they kept that thing going and now you could argue that there's a new generation that didn't know anybody on the other side in earlier times, but followed in the footsteps, adopted that same ethic of collaboration which is now carrying on the work. Meanwhile the politicians in Cyprus are still stuck and they still can't get along. So a lot of this professional work doesn't actually have much traction, but that's a beautiful model, and basically it's about individuals saying: 'It goes against my honour to stop talking to these people, even though my boss tells me I'm not allowed to talk to them and I'm not allowed to work with them'.

And so the famous story is that they would get together, unofficially on weekends in the buffer zone, to talk and share and tell jokes and all that good stuff and that's how they kept it going, so that's a beautiful kind of underground story and it's the only one of its kind I found in terms of divided cities. Obviously if you go to a place like Jerusalem, nothing like that happened at all, maybe a handful of Israeli planners who were very enlightened would talk to and worked a little bit with a handful of Palestinian planners, but almost not at all. In other places like Belfast it was much more mixed. Belfast didn't do the kind of beautiful inspiring direct unofficial mediation that they do still in Cyprus. Belfast is special because their education system is so fantastic, these people are just so beautifully educated in terms of their critical thinking ability that, in my opinion, what they did was something maybe even more interesting. They did critical studies about the cost of partition (Moriarty 1994). It's the best one I've ever seen: they look at every impact of partition: medical, psychological, employment, everything bad and good (but there's not much good) that came out of the Troubles and of the peace lines in Belfast. They use this beautiful education and analytical thinking to look at what the results were, what we really got out of this partition, and it's almost all hideously bad. In my opinion that's an admirable thing, because they refused to toe the party line and say: 'we must do this to protect ourselves'. A lot of these professionals said: 'No, this whole thing stinks to high heaven and we're going to show that we do not accept it'. Even if they have to accept it in their jobs, they would use every opportunity and every bit of funding they could find to look very critically at the impact of partition, and I can't think of another divided city scenario that looks as clearly and candidly at the actual impact, the measurable negative impact on regular people's lives as that study did. So, you have to love the fact that they maintained their professional integrity despite the compromises many of them had to make. Almost every city has some version of these problems, whether it's very latent or very obvious.

This is not an original statement, but just going back to the question of whether or not policy makers and built environment people could be having a more fruitful conversation, we certainly could, because we're talking about fundamental dynamics that either strengthen or undermine the health of struggling urban communities and that should be a very interesting subject to almost everybody. The fact that it isn't more of a conversation, that we don't consult each other more, is difficult to understand, because we can be doing so much more of a good job in many of these places long before there's a wall in place. There are these shiny glints of hope in the professional world, but in terms of how people have responded to and studied partition they're very few and I found the majority of professional groups to be passive, often fatalistic and sometimes enthusiastic participants in the partition.

S.F.:   *What are your current projects and what is puzzling you still about your work?*

J.C.:   I'm not working on these issues anymore. I wish I was, they're so important and we've just barely begun to understand them. I'm working on very different things at the moment that don't have to do with cities or partition, but I did spend a year studying the Roma camps outside Rome, Italy. I was looking at the gypsy camps, many of which are built by the Italian government. I went into those camps and I looked at the living conditions there trying to understand the political logic of building and maintaining these places for despised people. We all know that the Roma occupy the lowest rung on the ladder of social status in most parts of Europe, and I find that very important because the idea of the ghetto, the idea of the ethnic enclave that is mandated and maintained like an open air jail by a government – which was of course the product of medieval or Renaissance Italy – is a core concept. It is the idea that a government can take a group of people that it doesn't like and put them into a cage and use them like an object for directing the hatred of the majority.

There's so many different versions of ghetto, but I thought I would go back to the original prototype, the Jewish ghetto – and I was comparing the prototype of the Jewish ghetto of the sixteenth century with what I consider to be the new version, which is the Roma camp of today. That seed of the idea of urban partition, I firmly believe, was the Jewish ghetto in Venice of the sixteenth century. It was like a 'horribly brilliant' invention and unless we fully understand the brilliance and horribleness of that Jewish ghetto invention, we can't fully understand the persistence and the recurrence of urban ethnic partitions today, because they're very different and they've taken on all these new hybrid forms, but they share a lot.

The last work I did was trying to look at that original version and I found it to be very revealing.

It sheds a lot of light on the larger question of ethnic antagonism and partition in the domestic realm. We are wasting our time if we continue to fetishise the outward manifestations of these partitions. We're spending our time well if we push down towards the core questions and continue to look at basic issues of how they are hurting people over and over again on a daily basis. As people who are involved in the built environment, we're supposed to really care about those things.

And yet I don't feel like we're nearly bothered enough by it, and so many of us spend our time worrying about formal aesthetic details of wealthy cityscapes, when we have whole communities, societies, cities that are jut suffering under the pile-up of bad and even violent decisions that have been made. I feel like we should say 'first things first'. As a professional, before we worry about the elegant embroidery at the edge of something, let's look at the centre: is the centre strong or is it rotten?

I feel like these studies of the very dysfunctional cities shed light on the broader problem of how often we miss the most fundamental dynamics and conversations that are at the centre of what our profession is supposed to be about, which is making people live more prosperous lives.

S.F.:   We perhaps need a critical mass of pieces of work that speak in a certain way about the built environment and cities and partitions and make it relevant?

J.C.:   I agree with you, it is about reaching a tipping point each time another effort like yours takes place it builds towards this point. I don't feel like the work that's been done to date has yet had much of a positive impact on those actual people, but it could and this has got to be the sometimes frustrating path, that leads us to maybe being able to say that, at the end of the day, some bad thing was avoided, or some good thing was engineered because of the insights that were eventually collected in this way.

S.F.:   What are your current projects?

J.C.:   I'm living in a very small town called Eastport in Maine, which is one of the poorest states in the United States. We're looking at the problem of heating in the winter, so like I said, it's something completely different from all the things that I have been working on before. What we're looking at is how people without much money can get high efficiency heating systems put into schools and houses, so that they stop spending so much money which they really can't afford on heat. It's a very mundane problem, but it's a huge issue in the United States and in England, because people live in big leaky old houses that have bad furnaces, and so a group of colleagues and I got interested in why as architects we've failed so many people in this way in terms of the most basic thing, providing shelter, because people are really cold and they can't afford to heat themselves, in these parts of the country, so we started a project called 'Thermal Efficiency Eastport' and we decided to partner with this small community to see what we could do in a very representative place to address this question of equal access to basics.

In the same way, urban planners and others have essentially failed in their responsibility to help and protect the most vulnerable communities, with respect to urban partition, by ducking the hard questions. The same thing is true with architects, who instead of debating whether you like the tower in Dubai or hate the tower in Dubai, should be talking first about whether we're doing a good job bringing to the regular person the best thing we know how to do: a comfortable, safe, warm home. One of the things that motivated this project now is the question: How could we have missed something so basic?

Looking back, I suppose I had gone as far as I could go in terms of making any useful conversation to the whole urban partition thing and I just felt that it was not ultimately leading me into a place where I felt like I was being very useful, so with regret I turned to another subject that I care a lot about. There's a long way to go before the conversation about urban partition evolves to the point where there's any chance that it could impact policy and that's really got to be our goal, because that's where the problems stop and start.

S.F.:   *Thank you for this interview.*

LOOKING ACROSS

All of our interviewees seem to agree on the enormous relevance of materiality, ranging from large urban infrastructures to rather small, mundane and ordinary artefacts. Jon Calame, however, warns that we must not 'fetishise the outward manifestations of partitions'. He puts the most emphasis on political issues like power plays by political actors (local as well as international ones), who manipulate and instrumentalise the situation for their own gain. Calame identifies and blames their 'divide and conquer' approach as part of the 'initial infection' which must be tackled at least as importantly as their symptoms, that is, the material settings in conflict cities. We do not dispute this but would like to argue that such symptoms can also take on a life of their own and contribute to the momentum of a deteriorating situation.

But Calame is certainly not trying to downplay the importance of the urban environment. On the contrary, he, too, stresses the importance of seeing the big picture, which includes materiality. Wendy Pullan is even more explicit on this question: She does 'not want to diminish the importance of politics, but one of the things that is not taken into account are the urban aspects of the city'. She also emphasises that the whole issue is 'very spatial. It's, of course, social, but it's primarily spatial. Divided cities can't only be seen through social groups'. Scott Bollens calls this 'the power of urbanism' and emphasises that sometimes this power is being or can be used for better or worse.

Jon Calame agrees on the lack of attention to such issues by conventional decision-makers. He deplores their difficulty (at best) or ignorance (at worst) to take into account the concreteness of people's material lives. In his view they 'live in a world that is so policy-driven, very abstract, large scale, very much about diplomatic interactions, at a very esoteric level. They're so used to ingesting statistical data, they're not used to any kind of data coming in a different form' – like an analysis of the material and spatial aspects of conflict.

Interestingly, Calame doesn't only accuse mainstream conflict scholars and practitioners. His diagnosis also concerns 'built environment professionals' who can be rather 'inarticulate and almost illiterate in terms of policy. We don't speak the same languages … we just keep on talking to each other, it's like preaching to the choir, we don't make any serious effort to extend the meanings and the insights from our domain over the fences into other domains'.

The proactive involvement of practitioners in our project and the creation of a systematically de-jargonised touring exhibition was our attempt to counteract this common danger of scholarly parochialism.

In one way or another all our interviewees are interested in and study not only the *condition* of urban conflict but also in the *dynamics*, that is the trend towards and away from (violent) conflict; very close to what we call polarisation and radicalisation. For Jon Calame, the situation often resembles a 'pile of dry sticks' which do not necessarily inflame, unless some spark – which can be internal or external – sets them ablaze. We have encountered cases where the mere introduction of a seemingly innocent new material artefact (like the Westlink Bridge – see Chapter 3) acted as such a spark. Frank Gaffikin has very specific thoughts about the condition of escalation. He agrees that disagreements around territory can be among the key source of grievances and anger – however, not in the sense of an automatic trigger.

Almost all cities are characterised by a certain degree of disputes and controversies, but not all of them end up in inferno. All interviewees agree and therefore argue that the challenge is to deal with conflict in a civil fashion – to channel conflict into non-violent expressions. There is universal agreement that the solution cannot be to sweep difference under the carpet. Pullan, Gaffikin and Bollens are adamant about this – and Calame would probably be too had the conversation touched upon this point: Exposure to difference is actually very important. The challenge is to avoid the discourse slipping into a perceived binary alternative between winning or losing. This reminds us of a passage Frank Gaffikin and Ralf wrote a few years ago: We need to 'change from a politics of antagonism, where the opponent is perceived as an enemy to be crushed, to a politics of agonism, where the opponent is perceived as an adversary to be contested with, within a mutual acknowledgement of the right to differ' (Brand and Gaffikin 2007: 292). Wendy Pullan therefore reminds us that we must not just try to manage conflict – through built environment interventions or otherwise – but to think long-term and to tackle its root causes.

Another particularly interesting comment by Wendy Pullan alerts us to a common misconception: Traditionally, conflict is seen as something that takes place at the periphery, near the boundaries where nations in dispute meet. However, the situation in Israel/Palestine teaches us that conflict is played out in the heart of our cities. The frontier is in the middle of our societies. Analogous interpretations can help us better understand Islamic radicalisation, neo-Nazi radicalisation and other forms of extremism. And in all these cases, sometimes rather abstract, ideological and geopolitical disputes trickle into our streets and houses and trigger a silent adjustment of our daily lives. All our interviews highlight, only with different words, the importance to understand these habits and ingrained routines that develop as a consequence. After some time, most of them are out of reach from cognitive scrutiny and can turn the residents into some kind of somnambulists.

This is the starting point of a point made most explicitly by Calame and Bollens: As outsiders we have the unique benefit of a healthy distance to scan the situation in any given city. The outsider can see certain things that have already become normalised, domesticated and second nature to the insider. On the other hand, those who want to understand a certain complex local situation from the outside lack, almost by definition, the knowledge of all the intricacies that characterise any city. Despite such irresolvable professional dilemmas and trade-off we must not cease our attempts to get to grips with the phenomenon of polarised and polarising cities.

10

EPILOGUE
From Polarisation to Shared Spaces:
The Influence of the Built Environment in Contested Societies

Jon Coaffee

Urban planning and architectural design are increasingly seen as universal remedies to an ever-expanding array of socio-economic problems, policy priorities and risks and threats facing contemporary society. We are told that the role and remit of such built environment professions now includes dealing, for example, with climate change, obesity and well-being, social inclusion, as well as their formative role in balancing the social, economic and environmental impacts of development in all its guises (Coaffee 2009b). As this book, and other recent literature, has highlighted, such professions, although still underconsidered, are increasingly playing a role in countering the threat of international terrorism and associated radicalisation/ polarisation/violent extremism (Coaffee et al. 2009). Indeed, in recent years in the UK and across the European Union, counter-terrorism has increasingly focused on preventing radicalisation amongst populations as part of a 'softer' and more community-orientated form of proactive 'human' security policy. In the UK, the so-called PREVENT strand of the national counter-terrorism strategy (CONTEST), which was concerned with tackling the underlying causes of terrorism, particularly those linked to violent extremism, became central to work on national security following the devastating attacks on the London transport infrastructure on 7 July 2005. As Briggs (2010) noted, the *Prevent* strand has 'grown in stature relative to the other three strands (*Pursue*, *Protect* and *Prepare*); funding has increased from £6 million per year in 2006 to £140 million in 2008/9; and it is now being delivered by local authorities, community organizations and other groups' (971).

Where we can criticise the UK and European approaches – which both adopted this four-pronged strategy to counter-terrorism – was in the inability to consistently connect and coordinate action across the thematic areas of the overall strategy. The research unpacked in detail in this book represents one such attempt to undertake such joined-up thinking to the new security challenges facing contemporary society. What this work does, within the urban context of enhanced threat and counter-militarisation trends, is pose and then attempt to provide answers to a series of questions regarding how *Protect* and *Prevent* strands might influence each other, and civil society, through the design of the built environment. For example, it asks: What impact do visible security features or 'markers' of conflict have upon individual and group perceptions of public spaces or residential areas? Do they make people feel vulnerable, alienated or excluded? Can these feelings contribute to violent extremism? And, more specifically, can a fortress environment mirror 'radical' tendencies, and can a sensitively designed built environment help mediate them? (Coaffee 2010). In short the research undertaken for this book looks at the macro- and micro-design of the built environment simultaneously with urban form treated as an independent variable in potentially influencing behaviour.

Such a relationship between urban design, and violent or criminogenic environments, is not a new academic pursuit. Much post-war research in this area had its roots in ideas of 'defensible space' and 'design determinism' emanating from the United States in the late 1960s and early 1970s (see for example Newman 1972) and early attempts at behavioural geography in the 1980s, which focused upon the study of how cognitive processes were affected by, and responded to, the perceived environment. This work included topics such as environmental perception, cognitive mapping, and the development of attitudes about spaces and places. These studies were based on a premise that 'the way in which people behave is mediated by their understanding of the environments in which they live or with which they are confronted' (Gold 1980: frontispiece).

Subsequently, other strands of work, particularly in cultural geography and architectural studies, have portrayed urban landscapes as texts that can be 'read', revealing a range of interpretations of conflict, war and terrorism in a more culturally sensitive way where the urban landscape thus becomes 'a medium in which social relations and processes are formed and reproduced' (Daniels 1993: 1026). Landscapes, viewed through this conceptual lens, are thus moulded by politics and may be read as texts that 'reveal' the symbolic importance of their constituent elements (Coaffee et al. 2009). These and similar such 'textual' modes of analysis were employed to illuminate the upsurge in urban fear in the 1990s, recognising how the visual aesthetics came to symbolise conflict, violence and terror (see for example Davis 1995). Further studies have also highlighted how symbolic markers of territorial conflict – counter-terrorism features or memorials to conflicts – produce highly symbolic (and often contested) landscapes (Boal and Murray 1977; Coaffee et al. 2009; Johnson 1995). As highlighted in this book, this aspect is crucial to cities such as Belfast (Chapter 4) and particularly Beirut (Chapter 5). In the latter, it was observed how several scars of recent conflicts are purposely kept open through specific material interventions in the urban landscape: Shrines, memorials and even digital clocks scattered around the city, counting the days since the killing of specific public figures. As Neil Jarman (1993: 107) noted in relation to the residential and retail areas of Belfast from the early 1970s to the mid-1990s: 'The apparent permanence of the conflict and the lack of any solutions acceptable to all parties has meant that the ideological divisions have increasingly become a concrete part of the physical environment, creating an ever more militarised landscape.'

More recently, it has been proposed that such spatiality, specifically memorials to conflict, may function as a 'radical space of communication' as well as being a fixed moment for generating healing and/or didactic purposes (McKim 2008: 83; see also Bleiker 2006).

Traditional conceptions regarding conflict, contestation and terrorism have evolved to take account of an increasingly complex, interdependent and (we are told) potentially more threatening security environment. At the city scale, such trends are perhaps most apparent when the 'meaning' of security landscapes is contested by citizens. This gets to the heart of the research question central to this book – does the built environment mirror social contestation, or can the built environment be a mediating force in producing increasingly cohesive societies where radicalisation/polarisation is less likely?

Today, the visible (and increasingly invisible) moulding of the built environment is conducted because of social, political and economic priorities, some of which are associated with conflict, contestation, security and insecurity. As Bollens, in his work in post-conflict Barcelona, Bilbao, Mostar and Sarajevo, asked: What is the nature of the relationship between socio-political conditions and changes to urban materiality and space? Are interventions that manipulate urban materiality and space in ethnically contentious cities capable of advancing or retarding intergroup tolerance? (2009: 79). In a more extreme way Weizman has provided a forensic account of how architectures, both large and small in scale, have been utilised as instruments of control by the Israeli state against Palestinian communities. In *Hollow Land* he notes how 'overt instruments of control, as well as seemingly mundane structures, are pregnant with intense historical, political meaning' and how the politics is inscribed in architecture and 'solidify into the organisation, form and ornamentation of homes, infrastructure and settlements' (2007: 6). Moreover, as the broader 'War on Terror' narrative illustrates we cannot conceive the contemporary (Western) city without at least being aware of terror threats and in many respects seeking to 'design out' such vulnerabilities. As Graham has noted (2004: 171) this aptly illustrates 'the inseparability of war, terror and modern urbanism' with increasing attention now being paid to the complex and localised impact of defensive strategies upon social, political and economic life (Coaffee and Wood 2006).

It is clear that architecture and the built form more generally has the capacity to transmit a range of dominant ideologies, potentially illustrating how a particular society is materially inscribed into space (Ellin and Blakely 1997). Others have also argued that architecture and urban design have the power to order and control society through environmental determinism, with such embodied experiences often serving to in/exclude particular groups from certain spaces of the city. The built form then potentially possesses the power to condition new forms of subjectivity with spatial performances of identity and (in)security becoming linked to how subjects internalise fear or feel alienated from the 'mainstream' (Coaffee et al. 2009).

Drawing on a number of diverse case studies this research project has drawn attention to a range of mechanisms by which built environment professionals can engage productively within design, planning and architectural practices and processes. Given the social, political morphological and contextual complexity of the contested cities field, there are no 'silver bullet' design fixes that can be transferred from place to place without the 'receiving' city adapting ideas to specific time-space contexts. However, what this book has revealed are a myriad of ways in which the built form can impact upon the processes that might contribute to alienation, polarisation and in extreme cases radicalisation and violent extremism. Whilst such processes are perhaps highlighted in cities classically recognised as 'contested', they are also found in cities considered as 'relatively peaceful'. Moreover, this book highlights the increasingly sensitive ways that urban spaces might be designed so that they embrace principles of conviviality, inclusiveness and safety where citizens of different types encounter each other in a safe environment be it a street or commercial outlet. The flip side of this move towards a process on integrative planning are the segregated spaces with an absence of cultural integration that many posit can serve as breeding grounds for radical and violent tendencies. But, what formal role might built environment professionals play in this process of building more cohesive communities through engagement and cross-cultural activity?

Over recent decades the process and principles underpinning urban planning have been reappraised in light of the growing diversity and multiculturalism of cities as well as key protest and emancipation movements from working-class communities, immigrants, people of differing ethnicities and increasingly those representing communities of interest and identity. These groups have commonly protested about the destruction of their traditional living spaces and sought a greater voice within the planning process in order to influence decision-making. As Wood and Landry have noted, 'in a world of increasing mobility, how people of different cultures live together is a key issue of our age, especially for those responsible for planning and running cities' and as such 'new thinking is needed on how diverse communities can cooperate in productive harmony instead of leading parallel or antagonistic lives' (2007: frontispiece).

As theories of diversity and multiculturalism in the city have been developed so too has the potential for a plethora of different groupings to feed into the process of planning with planners and other built environment professionals such as architects and urban designers, increasingly seen as 'facilitators' between diverse groupings wishing to negotiate mutually inclusive planned outcomes.

This need for a better understanding and acknowledgement of diversity and multiculturalism in urban planning has been especially evident across Europe with waves of 'Islamophobia' that followed the terrorist attacks in New York and Washington, DC in September 2001 amidst largely unsubstantiated fears of particular urban neighbourhoods being breeding grounds for the radicalisation of Muslims (Allen 2010) or forms of far-right extremism (Goodwin 2007). As such, planning practice has increasingly sought to adopt more pluralistic approaches which are centred upon inclusivity, openness and equality in planning decision-making and especially the role that local citizens have to play in determining the material form and governance of the places in which they live. Here, as Healey (1988: 1546) notes, 'collaborative approaches emphasise the importance of building new policy discourses about the qualities of places, developing collaboration among stakeholders in policy development as well as delivery, widening stakeholder involvement beyond traditional power elites, recognising different forms of local knowledge, and building rich social networks as a resource of institutional capital through which new initiatives can be taken rapidly and legitimately'. In this respect collaborative modes of planning provide an 'inclusive dialogic approach to shaping social space' while featuring contemporary issues including 'reduced certitudes and predictabilities and … new modes of governance that acknowledges the need to involve multiple stakeholders' (Brand and Gaffikin 2007: 283). In practice a range of urban polices have emerged in response to diversity and increasing multiculturalism, which Fincher and Iveson (2008: 3) argue are based on a set of social logics planners can use to guide their actions:

1. redistribution – relating to the ambition of redressing disadvantages through for example regeneration and renewal schemes;
2. recognition – aiming to decrypt the profiles of hidden voices to better assess their needs, for example planning specific neighbourhoods or neighbourhood services for certain immigrant groups;
3. encounter – referring to the scope of plans for increasing an individual's opportunity to socialise through, for example, creating 'shared' or convivial' spaces where a variety of cultural encounters can occur (for example community shopping centres or community festivals).

Planning policies and social policy more broadly (including preventative counter-terrorism and security policy) has traditionally been focused upon mitigating the perceived negative effects of diversity and multiculturalism, with little thought given to the social and economic benefits of embracing diversity and in an enlightened move from multicultural society to one that embraces interculturalism (exchanges between cultural groups). Cultural change is required amongst the built environment professions, in order to better understand the important role that planning, urban design and architecture can play in helping tackle diversity and disadvantage. This can be done for example by assisting the revival of the most deprived neighbourhoods, reducing social exclusion and polarisation and supporting society's most vulnerable groups which are also those most likely to be radicalised (House of Commons 2012). Such enlightened professionalism is paramount in the evolution of the future city.

References

Adey, P. and Anderson, B. 2012. Anticipating emergencies: Technologies of preparedness and the matter of security. *Security Dialogue*, 43(2), 99–117.

Aibar, E. and Bijker, W.E. 1997. Constructing a City: The Cerda Plan for the Extension of Barcelona. *Science, Technology & Human Values*, 22(1), 3–30.

Akrich, M. 1992. The description of technical objects. In Wiebe E. Bijker and J. Law (eds), *Shaping technology/building society studies in sociotechnical change*, Cambridge, MA: MIT Press, 205–24.

Allen, C. 2010. *Islamophobia*, Farnham and Burlington: Ashgate.

Amnesty International. 2006. *Lebanon: Deliberate destruction or 'collateral damage'? Israeli attacks on civilian infrastructure*, Amnesty International. Available at: www.amnesty. org/en/library/asset/MDE18/007/2006/en/4a9b367a-d3ff-11dd-8743-d305bea2b2c7/ mde180072006en.pdf [accessed 25 July 2012].

Amsterdam-Slotervaart City Council. 2007. *Slotervaart action plan: Countering radicalisation*. Available at: www.nuansa.nl/uploads/5c/83/.../Slotervaart-plan-English.doc [accessed 24 July 2012].

Angel, S. 1968. *Discouraging crime through city planning*, Berkeley, CA: University of California Press.

Bakker, K. and Bridge, G. 2006. Material worlds? Resource geographies and the 'matter of nature'. *Progress in Human Geography*, 30(1), 5–27.

Bartels, E. and de Jong, I. 2008. Civil society on the move in Amsterdam: Mosque organizations in the Slotervaart district. *Journal of Muslim Minority Affairs*, 27(3), 455–71.

BBC News. 2012. *England riots: Plans to ease rules on shop shutters abandoned*. Available at: www.bbc.co.uk/news/uk-politics-19215375 [accessed 31 August 2012].

Beebeejaun, Y. 2009. Making safer places: Gender and the right to the city. *Security Journal*, 22(3), 219–29.

Beebeejaun, Y. 2010. Do multicultural cities help equality? In J.S. Davies and D.L. Imbroscio (eds), *Critical Urban Studies – New Directions*, Albany, NY: SUNY Press, 121–34.

Beebeejaun, Y. and Vanderhoven, D. 2010. Informalizing participation: Insights from Chicago and Johannesburg. *Planning Practice and Research*, 25(3), 283–96.

Bevan, R. 2005. *The destruction of memory: Architecture at war*, London: Reaktion.

Bijker, W.E. 1992. The social construction of fluorescent lighting, or how an artifact was invented in its diffusion state. In Wiebe E. Bijker and J. Law (eds), *Shaping technology/ building society studies in sociotechnical change*, Cambridge, MA: MIT Press, 75–102.

Bijker, W.E. and Law, J. (eds) 1992. *Shaping technology/building society studies in sociotechnical change*, Cambridge, MA: MIT Press.

Bleiker, R. 2006. Art after 9/11. *Alternatives: Global, Local, Political*, 31(1), 77–99.

Boal, F.W. and Murray, R.C. 1977. A city in conflict. *Geographical Magazine*, 49, 364–71.

Bogdanovic, B. 1994. The city and death. In Labon, J. (ed.), *Storm 6: Out of Yugoslavia*, London: Storm/Carcanet, 53–57.

Bollens, S. 1998a. Ethnic stability and urban reconstruction: Policy dilemmas in polarized cities. *Comparative Political Studies*, 31(6), 683–713.

Bollens, S. 1998b. Urban policy in ethnically polarized societies. *International Political Science Review*, 19(2), 187–215.

Bollens, S. 1999. *Urban peace building in divided societies – Belfast and Johannesburg*, Boulder: Westview Press.

Bollens, S. 2000. *On narrow ground: Urban policy and ethnic conflict in Jerusalem and Belfast*, Albany, NY: SUNY Press.

Bollens, S. 2002. Urban planning and intergroup conflict: Confronting a fractured public interest. *Journal of the American Planning Association*, 68(1), 22–42.

Bollens, S. 2006. Urban planning and peace building. *Progress in Planning*, 66(2), 67–139.

Bollens, S. 2007. *Cities, nationalism, and democratization*, Abingdon: Routledge.

Bollens, S. 2009. Intervening in politically turbulent cities: Spaces, buildings, and boundaries. *Journal of Urban Technology*, 16(2–3), 79–107.

Bollens, S. 2012. *City and soul in divided societies*, Abingdon: Routledge.

Bowcott, O. 2009. *Bored teenagers blamed as lurid graffiti makes comeback after attack at barracks. Guardian*. Available at: www.guardian.co.uk/uk/2009/mar/10/barracks-attack-graffiti [accessed 14 September 2009].

Brand, R. 2008. Co-evolution of technical and social change in action: Hasselt's approach to urban mobility. *Built Environment*, 34(2), 182–99.

Brand, R. 2009a. From the guest editor: The architecture of war and peace. *Journal of Urban Technology*, 16(2–3), 1–7.

Brand, R. 2009b. Urban artifacts and social practices in a contested city. *Journal of Urban Technology*, 16(2–3), 35–60.

Brand, R. 2009c. Written and unwritten building conventions in a contested city: The case of Belfast. *Urban Studies*, 46(12), 2669–89.

Brand, R. 2011. Polarisation takes place. *Shared Space: A Research Journal on Peace, Conflict and Community Relations in Northern Ireland*, 5(2), 17–27.

Brand, R. and Gaffikin, F. 2007. Collaborative planning in an uncollaborative world. *Planning Theory*, 6(3), 282–313.

Brand, R., Gaffikin, F., Morrissey, M. and Perry, D. 2008. *Changing the contested city, Belfast: Contested cities – urban universities*. Available at: www.webcitation.org/61qESyvJs [accessed 10 February 2012].

Briggs, R. 2010. Community engagement for counterterrorism: Lessons from the United Kingdom. *International Affairs*, 86(4), 971–81.

Brown, B. 1987. Territoriality. In D. Stokols and I. Altman (eds), *Handbook of environmental psychology*, Chicago: Wiley.

Buijs, F., Demant, F. and Hamdy, A. 2006. *Strijders van eigen bodem: radicale en democratische moslims in Nederland*, Amsterdam: Amsterdam University Press.

Calame, J. and Charlesworth, E. 2009. *Divided cities: Belfast, Beirut, Jerusalem, Mostar, and Nicosia*, Philadelphia: University of Pennsylvania Press.

Callon, M. 1996. Le Travail de la Conception en Architecture. *Situations, Les Cahiers de la Recherche Architecturale*, 37(1er trimestre), 25–35.

Cantle, T. 2001. *The Cantle Report – Community Cohesion: A report of the Independent Review Team*. Available at: http://resources.cohesioninstitute.org.uk/Publications/Documents/Document/DownloadDocumentsFile.aspx?recordId=96&file=PDFversion [accessed 13 March 2012].

Chaktoura, M. 2005. *La guerre des graffiti. Liban 1975–1977*, Beirut: Editions Dar an-Nahar.

Charlesworth, E. 2006. *Architects without frontiers: War, reconstruction and design responsibility*, Amsterdam and London: Architectural.

Chatzis, K. and Coutard, O. 2005. Water and gas: Early developments in the utility networks of Paris. *Journal of Urban Technology*, 12(3), 1–17.

Clapper, M. 2006. School design, site selection, and the political geography of race in postwar Philadelphia. *Journal of Planning History*, 5(3), 241–63.

Coaffee, J. 2003. *Terrorism, risk, and the city: The making of a contemporary urban landscape*, Aldershot and Burlington: Ashgate.

Coaffee, J. 2004. Rings of steel, rings of concrete and rings of confidence: Designing out terrorism in Central London pre and post September 11th. *International Journal of Urban and Regional Research*, 28(1), 201–11.

Coaffee, J. 2009a. *Terrorism, risk and the global city: Towards urban resilience*, Farnham: Ashgate.

Coaffee, J. 2009b. What is the role and responsibility of planners and urban designers? In *Proceeding of the Institute of Civil Engineers: Urban Design and Planning*, 162(DP1), 35–6.

Coaffee, J. 2010a. Protecting the urban: The dangers of planning for terrorism. *Theory, Culture & Society*, 26(7–8), 343–55.

Coaffee, J. 2010b. Protecting vulnerable cities: The UK's resilience response to defending everyday urban infrastructure. *International Affairs*, 86(4), 939–54.

Coaffee, J. and O'Hare, P. 2008. Urban resilience and national security: The role for planners. *Proceeding of the Institute of Civil Engineers: Urban Design and Planning*, 161(DP4), 171–82.

Coaffee, J. and Wood, D.M. 2006. Security is coming home: Rethinking scale and constructing resilience in the global urban response to terrorist risk. *International Relations*, 20(4), 503–17.

Coaffee, J., O'Hare, P. and Hawkesworth, M. 2009. The visibility of (in)security: The aesthetics of planning urban defences against terrorism. *Security Dialogue*, 40(4–5), 489–511.

Coaffee, J., Wood, D.M. and Rogers, P. 2008. *The everyday resilience of the city: How cities respond to terrorism and disaster*, Basingstoke: Palgrave Macmillan.

Communities and Local Government Committee. 2009. *New inquiry and call for evidence: Preventing violent extremism*. Available at: www.parliament.uk/business/committees/committees-archive/clg/clgpn090721pve/ [accessed 9 July 2012].

Coward, M. 2002. Community as heterogeneous ensemble: Mostar and multiculturalism. *Alternatives*, 27(1), 29–66.

Coward, M. 2004. Urbicide in Bosnia. In Graham, S. (ed.), *Cities, war and terrorism: Towards an urban geopolitics*, Oxford: Blackwell, 154–71.

Coward, M. 2006. Against anthropocentrism: The destruction of the built environment as a distinct form of political violence. *Review of International Studies*, 32(3), 419.

Coward, M. 2007. 'Urbicide' reconsidered. *Theory and Event*, 10(2). Available at: http://muse. jhu.edu/content/crossref/journals/theory_and_event/v010/10.2coward.html [accessed 29 August 2012].

Daniels, S. 1993. *Fields of vision: Landscape imagery and national identity in England and the United States*, Cambridge: Polity.

Davis, M. 1995. Fortress Los Angeles: The militarization of urban space. In P. Kasinitz (ed.), *Metropolis: Center and symbol of our times*, London: Macmillan, 355–68.

Deeb, L. 2011. *Leisurely Islam: Negotiating social space and morality*, Princeton: Princeton University Press.

Delpal, C. 2001. La corniche de Beyrouth: Nouvel espace public. *Annales de la recherche urbaine*, 91, 74–82.

Department for Communities and Local Government. 2007. *Preventing violent extremism pathfinder fund 2007/08*. Case studies. Available at: www.communities.gov.uk [accessed 27 February 2013].

Dovey, K. 1999. *Framing places: Mediating power in built form*, London and New York: Routledge.

Dumper, M. and Pullan, W. 2010. *Jerusalem: The cost of failure*, London: Chatham House. Available at: www.chathamhouse.org/sites/default/files/public/Research/Middle%20 East/bp0210jerusalem.pdf. [accessed 27 February 2013].

Economic and Social Research Council. 2007. Programme specification of New Security Challenges: 'Radicalisation' and Violence – A Critical Reassessment.

Ellin, N. and Blakely, E.J. 1997. *Architecture of fear*, New York: Princeton Architectural Press.

Evans, G. 2006. Foreword. In Charlesworth, E. 2006. *Architects without frontiers: War, reconstruction and design responsibility*, Amsterdam and London: Architectural.

Fawaz, M. and Deboulet, A. 2011. Contesting the legitimacy of urban restructuring and highways in Beirut's irregular settlements. In D. Davis and N. Libertun de Duren (eds), *Cities and sovereignty: Identity politics in urban spaces*, Bloomington: Indiana University Press, 117–51.

Fawaz, M. and Peillen, I. 2003. *Urban slums reports: The case of Beirut, Lebanon, understanding slums: Case studies for the Global Report on Human Settlements*. Available at: http://www. ucl.ac.uk/dpu-projects/Global_Report/pdfs/Beirut.pdf [accessed 27 February 2012].

Fincher, R. and Iveson, K. 2008. *Planning and diversity in the city: Redistribution, recognition and encounter*, Basingstoke: Palgrave.

Fregonese, S. 2008. *City, war and geopolitics: The relations between militia political violence and the built environment of Beirut in the early phases of the Lebanese civil war (1975–1976)*. Doctoral thesis. Newcastle upon Tyne: Newcastle University. Available at: http://ethos. bl.uk/OrderDetails.do?uin=uk.bl.ethos.492102 [accessed 3 September 2012].

Fregonese, S. 2009. The urbicide of Beirut? Geopolitics and the built environment in the Lebanese civil war (1975–1976). *Political Geography*, 28(5), 309–18.

Fregonese, S. 2012a. Between a refuge and a battleground: Beirut's discrepant cosmopolitanisms. *Geographical Review*, 102(3), 316–36.

Fregonese, S. 2012b. Beyond the 'weak state': Hybrid sovereignties in Beirut. *Environment and Planning D: Society and Space*, 30(4), 655–74.

Fregonese, S. 2013. Mediterranean Geographies of Protest. *European Urban and Regional Studies*, 20(1), 109–14.

Fregonese, S., forthcoming. *War and the city: Urban geopolitics in Lebanon*, London: IB Tauris.

Fregonese, S. and Brand, R. 2009. Polarisation as sociomaterial phenomenon: A bibliographical review. *Journal of Urban Technology*, 16(2–3), 9–34.

Gaffikin, F. and Morrissey, M. 2011. *Planning in divided cities*, Oxford: Wiley-Blackwell.

Ganapati, S. 2008. Critical appraisal of three ideas for community development in the United States. *Journal of Planning Education and Research*, 27(4), 382–99.

Githens-Mazer, J. 2008. Variations on a theme: Radical violent Islamism and European North African radicalization. *PS: Political Science & Politics*, 41(1), 19–24.

Glasze, G. 2003. Segmented governance patterns. Fragmented urbanism: The development of guarded housing estates in Lebanon. *The Arab World Geographer*, 6(2), 79–100.

Gold, J.R. 1980. *An introduction to behavioural geography*, Oxford and New York: Oxford University Press.

Gold, J.R. and Revill, G. 2000. *Landscapes of defence*, Harlow and New York: Prentice Hall.

Goodwin, M.J. 2007. The extreme right in Britain: Still an 'ugly duckling' but for how long? *The Political Quarterly*, 78(2), 241–50.

Gordon, D. 2012. *Could babies' faces reduce crime? BBC News*. Available at: www.bbc.co.uk/news/magazine-19398580 [accessed 31 August 2012].

Graham, S. 2001. The city as sociotechnical process: Networked mobilities and urban social inequalities. *City*, 5(3), 339–49.

Graham, S. 2004. *Cities, war, and terrorism: Towards an urban geopolitics*, Malden, MA: Blackwell.

Graham, S. 2006. Cities and the 'war on terror'. *International Journal of Urban and Regional Research*, 30(2), 255–76.

Graham, S. 2010. *Cities under siege: The new military urbanism*, London: Verso.

Gregory, D. and Pred, A. 2007. *Violent geographies: Fear, terror, and political violence*, New York: Routledge.

Guy, S. and Moore, S. 2005. *Sustainable architectures: Natures and cultures in Europe and North America*, London: Routledge.

Guy, S., Marvin, S. and Moss, T. 2001. *Urban infrastructure in transition: Networks, buildings, plans*, London and Sterling: Earthscan.

Haraway, D.J. 1991. *Simians, cyborgs and women: The reinvention of nature*, London: Free Association.

Healey, P. 1997. *Collaborative planning*, New York: Palgrave.

Healey, P. 1998. Building institutional capacity through collaborative approaches to urban planning. *Environment and Planning A*, 30(9), 1531–46.

Heimsath, C. 1977. *Behavioral architecture: Toward an accountable design process*, New York: McGraw-Hill.

HM Government. 2006. *Countering international terrorism: The United Kingdom's strategy*. Available at: www.iwar.org.uk/homesec/resources/uk-threat-level/uk-counterterrorism-strategy.pdf [accessed 14 February 2012].

HM Government. 2008. *Preventing violent extremism: A strategy for delivery*.

Hommels, A. 2005. *Unbuilding cities: Obduracy in urban socio-technical change*, Cambridge, MA: MIT Press.

Horgan, J. 2008. From profiles to pathways and roots to routes: Perspectives from psychology on radicalization into terrorism. *The ANNALS of the American Academy of Political and Social Science*, 618(1), 80–94.

Hoskins, A., Akil, A. and O'Loughlin, B. 2011. *Radicalisation and media connectivity and terrorism in the new media ecology*, London: Routledge.

Houdart, S. 2006. Des multiples manieres d'être reel: les representations en perspective dans le projet d'architecture. *Terrain*, 46(2006), 107–22.

House of Commons. 2012. *Roots of violent radicalisation*, London: TSO.

Hughes, T.P. 1983. *Networks of power: Electrification in Western society, 1880–1930*, Baltimore: Johns Hopkins University Press.

Hughes, T.P. 1988. The seamless web: Technology, science, etcetera, etcetera. *Social Studies of Science*, 16(2), 281–92.

Human Rights Watch. 2006. *Israel's Indiscriminate Attacks against Civilians in Lebanon*, Human Rights Watch. Available at: www.hrw.org/sites/default/files/reports/lebanon 0806webwcover.pdf [accessed 25 July 2012].

Hunter, W. 2008. Debate rejects call for counter-terrorism design. *BD: The Architects' Website*. Available at: www.bdonline.co.uk/comment/debate-rejects-call-for-counter-terrorism-design/3116938.article [accessed 20 March 2009].

Isin, E.F. 2002. *Being political: Genealogies of citizenship*, Minneapolis: University of Minnesota Press.

Jackson, P. 2000. Rematerializing social and cultural geography. *Social & Cultural Geography*, 1(1), 9–14.

Jacobs, J. 1961. *The death and life of great American cities*, New York: Random House.

Jacobs, J. 1964. *The death and life of great American cities the failure of town planning*, Harmondsworth: Penguin.

Jarman, N. 1993. Intersecting Belfast. In B. Bender (ed.), *Landscape: Politics and perspectives*, Oxford: Berg, 107–38.

Jeffery, C.R. 1971. *Crime prevention through environmental design*, Beverly Hills: Sage Publications.

Jeffery, C.R. 1977. *Crime prevention through environmental design*, Beverly Hills: Sage Publications.

Johnson, N. 1995. Cast in stone: Monuments, geography, and nationalism. *Environment and Planning D: Society and Space*, 13(1), 51–65.

Kabbani, O. 1998. Public space as infrastructure: The case of the postwar reconstruction of Beirut. In Rowe, P. and Sarkis, H. (eds), *Projecting Beirut: Episodes in the construction and reconstruction of a modern city*, Prestel: London, 240–59.

Kaldor, M. 1999. *New and old wars: Organized violence in a global era*, Cambridge: Polity Press.

Keith, M. 2005. *After the cosmopolitan? Multicultural cities and the future of racism*, London: Routledge.

Kirby, A. 2007. The London bombers as 'self-starters': A case study in indigenous radicalization and the emergence of autonomous cliques. *Studies in Conflict & Terrorism*, 30(5), 415–28.

Labaki, B. and Abou Rjeily, K. 1993. *Bilan des guerres du Liban, 1975–1990*, Paris: L'Harmattan.

Latour, B. 1992. Where are the missing masses? The sociology of a few mundane artifacts. In Wiebe E. Bijker and J. Law (eds), *Shaping technology/building society studies in sociotechnical change*, Cambridge, MA: MIT Press, 225–64.

Latour, B. 1993. On technical mediation: The Messenger Lectures on the Evolution of Civilization, *Institute of Economic Research, Working Papers Series*. Ithaca: Cornell University, Institute of Economic Research.

Latour, B. 1998. *Paris: Ville Invisible*, Paris: Les Empecheurs de Penser en Rond.

Latour, B. 2005. *Reassembling the social: An introduction to actor-network-theory*, Oxford and New York: Oxford University Press.

Lazell, M. 2009. Security Minister Adam West urges architects to 'design out' terrorism. *BD: The Architects' Website*. Available at: www.bdonline.co.uk/news/security-minister-adam-west-urges-architects-to-"design-out"-terrorism/3132776.article [accessed 20 March 2009].

Lees, L. 2002. Rematerializing geography: The 'new' urban geography. *Progress in Human Geography*, 26(1), 101–12.

Leonard, M. 2008. Building, Bolstering and Bridging Boundaries: Teenagers' Negotiations of Interface Areas in Belfast. *Journal of Ethnic and Migration Studies*, 34(3), 471–89.

Lindqvist, S. 2002. *A history of bombing*, London: Granta.

Luzar, C. Wagner, B., Borstel, D. and Landgraf, G. 2006. *Rechtsextremismus in der Weitlingstraße – Mythos oder Realität. Problemaufriss im Berliner Bezirk Lichtenberg.* Available at: www.zentrum-demokratische-kultur.de/app/so.asp?o=/_obj/EC5BA53B-593A-4C63-A891-988C982CB43F/inline/Studie-Lichtenberg-Weitlingstrasse_2006.pdf [accessed 24 April 2012].

Maasri, Z. 2008. *Off the wall: Political posters of the Lebanese civil war*, London: I.B. Tauris.

McCauley, C. and Moskalenko, S. 2008. Mechanisms of political radicalization: Pathways toward terrorism. *Terrorism and Political Violence*, 20(3), 415–33.

McKim, J. 2008. Agamben at Ground Zero: A memorial without content. *Theory, Culture & Society*, 25(5), 83–103.

Mele, C. 2012. Neoliberalism, race and the redefining of urban redevelopment. *International Journal of Urban and Regional Research*, 37(2), 598–617.

Metropolitan Police. 2012. *What is suspicious activity?* Available at: http://content.met.police.uk/Article/What-Is-Suspicious-Activity/1400006267719/14000062677190 (archived by WebCite® at www.webcitation.org/69lfc2C0B) [accessed 8 August 2012].

Miessen, M. and Basar, S. (eds) 2004. *Did someone say participate? An atlas of spatial practice*, Boston: MIT Press.

Ministry of Security and Justice. 2011. National Counterterrorism Strategy 2011–2015.

Moore, S.A. 2001. *Technology and place: Sustainable architecture and the Blueprint Farm*, Austin: University of Texas Press.

Moore, S. 2004. *Sustainable architectures*, London: Spon.

Moore, S.A. and Brand, R. 2003. The banks of Frankfurt and the sustainable city. *The Journal of Architecture*, 8(1), 3–24.

Moore, S.A. and Karvonen, A. 2008. Sustainable architecture in context: STS and design thinking. *Science Studies*, 21(1), 29–46.

Moriarty, M. 1994. The cost of partition. *International Review of Applied Economics*, 8(1), 95–9.

Morrissey, M. and Gaffikin, F. 2006. Planning for peace in contested space. *International Journal of Urban and Regional Research*, 30(4), 873–93.

Mostar Architects Association. 1993. Mostar '92 – urbicide. *Spazio e Società/Space and Society*, 16(62), 8–25.

Municipality of Amsterdam. 2007. Amsterdam against radicalisation. Available at: http://www.google.co.uk/url?sa=t&rct=j&q=amsterdam%20against%20radicalisation&source=web&cd=1&ved=0CF8QFjAA&url=http%3A%2F%2Fwww.eenveiligamsterdam.nl%2Fpublish%2Fpages%2F164993%2Famsterdam_against_radicalisation.pdf&ei=TtgPUKSpAcfZ0QWCk4DwDA&usg=AFQjCNFs33amNR4QDRTJeJ_Dak0yk6lY7A [accessed 25 July 2012].

Murphy, M. 2004. Glimpses of a future architecture. In Miessen, M. and Basar, S. (eds), *Did someone say participate? An atlas of spatial practice*, Cambridge, MA: MIT Press.

Musterd, S. and Ostendorf, W. 1998. *Urban segregation and the welfare state: Inequality and exclusion in western cities*, London: Routledge.

Newman, O. 1972. *Defensible space: Crime prevention through urban design*, New York: Macmillan.

Northern Ireland News. 2007. *Westlink Bridge opens sectarian attack route*. Northern Ireland News. Available at: www.4ni.co.uk/northern_ireland_news.asp?id=69549 [accessed 10 April 2008].

O'Duffy, B. 2008. Radical atmosphere: Explaining jihadist radicalization in the UK. *PS: Political Science & Politics*, 41(1), 37–42.

OED Online. 2012a. Mediate, v. *Oxford English Dictionary*. Available at: www.oed.com/view/En try/115659?isAdvanced=false&result=2&rskey=gLd6Ka& [accessed 27 February 2013].

OED Online. 2012b. Polarization, n. *Oxford English Dictionary*. Available at: www.oed.com/ view/Entry/146757?redirectedFrom=polarization [accessed 27 February 2013].

Oliver, J.E. 2010. *The paradoxes of integration: Race, neighborhood and civic life in multiethnic America*, Chicago: University of Chicago Press.

Peters, R. 1996. Our soldiers, their cities. *Parameters*, 26, 43–50.

Pinch, T.J. and Bijker, W.E. 1984. The social construction of facts and artefacts: Or how the sociology of science and the sociology of technology might benefit each other. *Social Studies of Science*, 14(3), 399–441.

Planergemeinschaft. 2008. *Stadtbild Agentur e. V. – Der Verein für den Weitlingkiez*. Available at: www.planergemeinschaft.de/sul/verein/index.htm [accessed 24 April 2012].

Press, D.G. 1999. Urban warfare: Options, problems, and the future. *Marine Corps Gazette*, 83(4), 14–33.

Pullan, W. 2006. Locating the civic in the frontier: Damascus Gate. In Miessen, M. and Basar, S. (eds), *Did someone say participate? An atlas of spatial practice*, Cambridge, MA: MIT Press.

Pullan, W., Misselwitz, P., Nasrallah, R. and Yacobi, H. 2007. Jerusalem's Road 1. *City*, 11(2), 176–98.

Putnam, R.D. 2007. E pluribus unum: Diversity and community in the twenty-first century: The 2006 Johan Skytte Prize Lecture. *Scandinavian Political Studies*, 30(2), 137–74.

Ramadan, A. 2009. Destroying Nahr el-Bared: Sovereignty and urbicide in the space of exception. *Political Geography*, 28(3), 153–63.

Ramadan, A. 2013. From Tahrir to the world: The camp as a political public space. *European Urban and Regional Studies*, 20(1), 145–9.

Rohracher, H. and Orbetzeder, M. 2002. Green buildings in context: Improving social learning processes between users and produces. *Built Environment*, 28(1), 73–84.

Roseman, C.C., Laux, H.-D. and Thieme, G. 1996. *EthniCity: Geographic perspectives on ethnic change in modern cities*, Lanham: Rowman & Littlefield.

Ryan, J. 2007. The four p-words of militant Islamist radicalization and recruitment: Persecution, precedent, piety, and perseverance. *Studies in Conflict & Terrorism*, 30(11), 985–1011.

Sageman, M. 2008. A strategy for fighting international Islamist terrorists. *The ANNALS of the American Academy of Political and Social Science*, 618(1), 223–31.

Schmid, C. 2008. Far right violence in Berlin – 2003 until 2006. University of Manchester – URBE Stakeholder workshop. Unpublished Powerpoint presentation.

Schön, D. 1987. *Educating the reflective practitioner*, San Francisco: Jossey-Bass.

Shaftoe, H. 2008. *Convivial urban spaces creating effective public places*, London and Sterling: Earthscan in association with the International Institute for Environment and Development. Available at: http://public.eblib.com/EBLPublic/PublicView.do?ptiID=430 178 [accessed 29 August 2012].

Slootman, M. and Tillie, J. 2006. *Processes of radicalisation: Why some Amsterdam Muslims become radicals*, Amsterdam: Institute for Migration and Ethnic Studies. Universiteit van Amsterdam.

Söderström, O. 2000. *Des Images pour Agir: Le Visuel en Urbanisme*, Lausanne: Payot.

Thrift, N. 2007. Immaculate warfare? The spatial politics of extreme violence. In Gregory, D. and Pred, A. (eds), *Violent geographies: Fear, terror, and political violence*, New York: Routledge, 273–94.

Till, K.E. 1999. Staging the past: Landscape designs, cultural identity and Erinnerungspolitik at Berlin's Neue Wache. *Cultural Geographies*, 6(3), 251–83.

Travis, A. 2006. Summer of race riots' feared after clashes in 2001. Available at: www.guardian. co.uk/politics/2006/dec/28/communities.freedomofinformation [accessed 14 February 2012].

Varady, D. 2008. Muslim residential clustering and political radicalism. *Housing Studies*, 23(1), 45–66.

Veldhuis, T. and Bakker, E. 2009. Muslims in the Netherlands: Tensions and violent conflict. In M. Emerson and O. Roy (eds), *Ethno-religious conflict in Europe: Typologies of radicalisation in Europe's Muslim communities*, Brussels: CEPS, 81–108.

Verbeek, P.P. 2005. *What things do: Philosophical reflections on technology, agency, and design*, University Park: Pennsylvania State University Press.

Verfassungsschutz Berlin. 2007. *Rechte Gewalt in Berlin 2003–2006*, Berlin: Staatsverwaltung für Inneres und Sport. Available at: www.berlin.de/imperia/md/content/seninn/ verfassungsschutz/fokus_rechte_gewalt_2003_bis_2006.pdf [accessed 27 February 2013].

Wallach, Y. 2013. The politics of non-iconic space. Sushi, shisha, and a civic promise in the 2011 Summer protests in Israel. *European Urban and Regional Studies*, 20(1), 150–54.

Warburton, D. 1998. Willem Breuker Kollektief. *Paris Transatlantic archives*. Available at: www. paristransatlantic.com/magazine/archives/dutchscene.html [accessed 25 July 2012].

Watson, S. 2006. *City publics: The (dis)enchantments of urban encounters*, London and New York: Routledge.

Weimann, G. and von Knop, K. 2008. Applying the notion of noise to countering online terrorism. *Studies in Conflict & Terrorism*, 31(10), 883–902.

Weinberg, L. and Pedahzur, A. 2003. *Political parties and terrorist groups*, London and New York: Routledge.

Weinberg, L. and Pedahzur, A. 2004. *Religious fundamentalism and political extremism*, London and Portland: Frank Cass.

Weizman, E. 2004. Strategic points, flexible lines, tense surfaces, and political volumes: Ariel Sharon and the geometry of occupation. In Graham, S. (ed.), *Cities, war, and terrorism: Towards an urban geopolitics*, Malden: Blackwell, 172–91.

Weizman, E. 2007. *Hollow land: Israel's architecture of occupation*, London and New York: Verso.

Wiedemann, E. 2007. The end of tolerance in Amsterdam. *New York Times*. Available at: www. nytimes.com/2007/08/02/world/europe/02spiegel.html?pagewanted=all [accessed 16 March 2012].

Winner, L. 1993. Upon opening the black box and finding it empty: Social constructivism and the philosophy of technology. *Science, Technology & Human Values*, 18(3), 362–78.

Wood, E. 1961. *Housing design: A social theory*, New York: Citizens' Housing and Planning Counsel of New York.

Wood, P. and Landry, C. 2007. *The intercultural city: Planning to make the most of diversity*, London: Earthscan.

Yaneva, A. 2005. Scaling up and down: Extraction trials in architectural design. *Social Studies of Science*, 35(6), 867–94.

Yiftachel, O. 1998. Planning and social control: Exploring the dark side. *Journal of Planning Literature*, 12(4), 395–406.

Index

Page numbers in *italics* refer to figures.